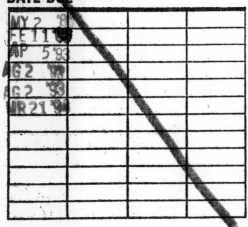

Styles of
Fashion

Styles of Fashion

A Pictorial Handbook

Mary D. Tranquillo

Illustrations by Suzanne Beall
Photography by Roula Liakos

 Van Nostrand Reinhold Company

New York Cincinnati Toronto London Melbourne

Printed in the United States of America

Designed by Sharen DuGoff Egana

Published by Van Nostrand Reinhold
Company Inc.
135 West 50th Street
New York, New York 10020

Van Nostrand Reinhold Company
Limited
Molly Millars Lane
Wokingham, Berkshire RG11 2PY,
England

Van Nostrand Reinhold
480 La Trobe Street
Melbourne, Victoria 3000, Australia

Macmillan of Canada
Division of Gage Publishing Limited
164 Commander Boulevard
Agincourt, Ontario M1S 3C7, Canada

16 15 14 13 12 11 10 9 8 7 6 5 4 3 2 1

**Library of Congress Cataloging in
Publication Data**

Tranquillo, Mary D.
  Styles of fashion.

  Bibliography: p.
  Includes index.
1. Clothing and dress—Handbooks,
manuals, etc.
2. Fashion—Handbooks, manuals, etc.
  I. Title.
TT515.T73   1984   391'.2
      83-21618
ISBN 0-442-28305-9

To
Joe,
Maria,
and all my students

Contents

Preface

Fashion constantly changes, but fashion styles are continually repeated. Each time a particular style is repeated, it is usually modified in some way to make it distinctive for a particular era. Sometimes the style is even given a different name. This constant change makes the fashion business fun, but it can also make accurately identifying a style frustrating. *Styles of Fashion* was written for you—the student, the professional, or the consumer of fashion—as an easy-to-use reference guide that will help you develop a command of the vocabulary of style.

Anyone who works with or uses fashion can benefit from a clear understanding of fashion terminology, and the drawings and photographs that accompany each definition in this book are invaluable learning aids. For the student and professional, *Styles of Fashion* will be useful for writing and delivering advertising copy, fashion-show commentary, sales presentations, and all types of sales and promotional work. The fashion director can use it to report style trends. The designer, design student, and fashion illustrator will all find the book a great source of inspiration. Last but not least, consumers will learn to identify the names of styles they may wish to adopt.

Styles of Fashion includes men's, women's, and children's styles. Each term is described and accompanied by alternative terms or modification, if appropriate. Also given is the time period in which the style was popular. Terms that are difficult to pronounce are accompanied by a phonetic spelling.

The terms selected for this book are the ones most commonly used during the twentieth century. The final section, Historical Silhouettes, covers the historical periods of fashion, beginning with antiquity and extending through the 1980s.

How To Use This Book

The book is divided into ten topic categories. Each style term under a particular topic is listed alphabetically. You can locate a specific term by looking under the topic or by checking the index (terms are arranged alphabetically in the index). To locate a term by topic, look under the topic first. For example, to find the term *polo shirt*, look in Section 3, Above-the-Waist Apparel. Check the main categories until you find *shirt* and then look for *polo* within that category.

Acknowledgments

My thanks to all my students, colleagues, and business acquaintances, who gave me so much encouragement. Special thanks go to typists Barbara Wales, Lorraine Heitman, Shirley Clement, and Margarita Busciglio, and to my editor, Susan Gies.

1
Active Sportswear

Bathing Suits
Bathing Suit Coverups
Dancewear
Equestrian Outfits
Hunting Outfits
Golf Outfits
Jogging Outfits
Tennis Outfits
Racquetball Wear
Skating Outfits
Skiwear
Sportswear Fabrics

Bathing Suits

Apparel worn by men, women, and children for swimming or sunbathing.

bikini
Very brief suit worn by men and women. Women's suit contains a brief bralike top and narrow bottom usually cut below the navel. Some designs connect the bottom front and back sections with a narrow string at sides. Men's suit is one brief bottom piece. Popular in 1960s, 1970s, and 1980s.

blouson (bloo-*sohn*)
One- or two-piece swimsuit worn by women. Top gathers below waistline, forming fullness over abdomen and hips.

boxer shorts
Wide, square-leg trunks used by men; waist usually elasticized. Classic style from the 1950s through the 1980s.

boy leg
Square leg used on women's and children's one- or two-piece swimsuits. A classic style during the 1970s and 1980s.

dressmaker
One-piece women's suit with skirt attached. Usually worn by mature women.

French-cut leg
Women's one-piece suit with very high cut leg. Very fashionable in 1970s and 1980s.

Gay '90s
A fad style of the 1960s that was adapted from men's knitted jersey underwear of the 1890s; usually made of horizontal stripe knit; sometimes one piece or two piece with tank top and narrow, knee-length pants.

jams
Men's suit that resembles cutoff pajamas with midthigh length and drawstring waist closing; usually made in colorful prints or stripes. Fashionable in the 1960s.

maillot (my-*yo*)
Form-fitting one-piece suit worn by women and children. Usually made of stretch-knit fabric without a skirt section. A classic style since 1930.

racing suit
Form-fitting knitted two-piece swimsuit worn by men in the 1920s and 1930s. Made popular by Johnny Weissmuller, Olympic swimmer.

sarong
Wrap-style swimsuit worn by women. Usually a one-piece maillot. Fashionable in 1970s and 1980s.

tank
Tight-fitting suit used by men, women, and children, particularly for swimming competition. Neckline on women's and children's is usually scooped with narrow straps at shoulder. Women's is distinguished from maillot by absence of under bra.

topless
Fad of the 1960s designed for shock appeal. Bottom was connected to top with narrow straps. Bill Blass and Rudi Gernrich were two of the most famous American designers to introduce it.

trunks
Men's shorts with boxy leg; vary in length from knee to very short. Used for surfing and swimming. Similar to boxer shorts but usually have narrower legs.

women's bikini.

boy leg.

jams.

sarong.

men's bikini.

dressmaker suit.

maillot.

women's tank suit.

blouson suit.

Gay '90s suit.

topless suit.

men's tank suit.

boxer shorts.

French-cut leg.

racing suit.

trunks.

Bathing Suit Coverups

Any apparel worn over or with a bathing suit to cover or complement it.

cabana set
Swimsuit and coordinating jacket worn by men. Coverup usually has patch pockets. Sometimes suit and jacket are made of identical fabrics; sometimes jacket is made of terry cloth and coordinated in color or trim with swimsuit.

caftan
Long, flowing garment that generally pulls over the head; usually worn by women.

cape
A circle or semicircle of fabric with hole cut for the head; sometimes opening is cut at center front to make it easier to put on.

drawstring top
Any style coverup that fastens with string at neck or bottom. Drawstring forms gathered softness when pulled.

elasticized dress *and* skirt
A rectangle of fabric with a casing of elastic at one end. Usually worn by women and children. A large rectangle would be used for the dress; a smaller rectangle for the skirt.

Pucci shirt
An overblouse with square bottom, tailored collar, and usually a brightly colored panel print. Originally designed by Italian designer Emilio Pucci. Widely imitated.

wrap jacket
Hip-length jacket with crossover front closing; usually held together with tie belt. Any neckline or collar may be used. Most frequently has banded neckline and is collarless.

Dancewear

Apparel worn by men, women, and children for ballet, tap, jazz, and acrobatic dancing, primarily because it allows for ease of movement. Also worn for exercising.

leotard
One-piece, form-fitting knitted garment that may have long, short, or no sleeves. Necklines and body styles vary. Named for nineteenth-century French aerial gymnast Jules Léotard. Used by male and female dancers. Usually worn with matching-color tights. Ballet dancers wear delicate pink-color tights and ballet slippers.

cabana set.

elasticized dress and skirt.

leotard.

caftan.

Pucci shirt.

leotard.

cape.

leotard.

drawstring top.

wrap jacket.

leotard.

leotard.

Equestrian Outfits

Costumes worn by men and women for horseback riding and related sports. Usually consist of a jacket, jodhpurs, and cap. Jackets can be short or long. Jodhpurs are wide at the hip and taper to a narrow hem at the ankles. The riding boot is pictured under *Boots*.

Hunting Outfits

For formal hunt meets, costume is similar to riding costume, with a bright red fabric used in the jacket. Informal hunting attire features a flannel single-breasted jacket and riding-type pants. The jacket is freqently made of a plaid fabric.

hunting outfit.

equestrian outfit.

equestrian outfit.

equestrian outfit.

Golf Outfits

Women's: usually comfortable pants or a culotte skirt with pockets, and a knitted T-shirt.

Men's: long or short pants and co-ordinating knit shirt.

Both men and women wear close-toed oxfords with spikes on the sole.

women's golf outfit.

men's golf outfit.

Jogging Outfits

Unisex garments worn for this popular sport of the 1960s, 1970s, and 1980s. For warm weather, shorts and tank-top jerseys are worn. Shorts have slits at side for ease of movement. In cold weather a warm-up suit is worn; has elasticized or drawstring waist, elasticized or straight-leg bottoms, and zippered front or pullover top. Jogging suits are made of velour, terry cloth, or fleece jersey knit. Shoe is a special type of sneaker that has an extra-thick cushioned sole.

women's jogging outfit.

men's jogging outfit.

Tennis Outfits

Attire can be unisex in design or different designs. Women wear short dresses with matching pants. Men (and sometimes women) wear short shorts and knitted sport shirts. Both traditionally made of white fabric. Matching white sneakers worn.

women's tennis outfit.

men's tennis outfit.

Racquetball Wear

Garments worn for this very popular sport of 1970s and 1980s are similar to warm-weather jogging suits. The styles are usually unisex in design.

women's racquetball outfit.

men's racquetball outfit.

Skating Outfits

Females wear a form-fitting dress with short, full skirt and tights. Males wear a form-fitting jumpsuit.

skating outfit.

Skiwear

Ski items include hood, jacket, vest, and pants. Pants, jackets, and vests are frequently made of windproof, lightweight fabric. Down-filled quilted items popular in the 1970s and 1980s. Pants usually have a strap at bottom to hold pant over the foot. Ski apparel usually of unisex designs.

skiwear.

Sportswear Fabrics

Fabrics used for sportswear are durable. Comfort and ease of movement are also important considerations when choosing a sportswear fabric. Color and pattern are often cheerful and bold.

argyle knit
Colorful, knitted, diamond-shaped plaid; popular in 1930s and 1960s for golf socks and sweaters.

brushed jersey
A plain knit fabric with a napped, fuzzy surface. Usually used for warm-up suits and bathing-suit coverups.

LaCoste knit
A textured double knit made of 100 percent cotton, 100 percent polyester or a combination of cotton and polyester; generally used for sports apparel and named after the manufacturer that made knit shirts popular. LaCoste knit sport shirts also have the recognizable alligator appliqué over the left chest.

patterned jersey
A single-knit fabric with the design knitted into construction. Back side is characterized by yarn floats. Used for a variety of sports apparel.

rib knit
Design is created by alternating knit and purl stitches. Has good stretch in the width direction. Used for the band or on entire wardrobe of sports-apparel items.

sateen
A semilustrous cotton or cotton blend made with a satin weave. Medium-weight fabric is used for sport shirts, shorts, and coverups.

stretch tricot
Warp knit fabric with spandex stretch yarns. Used for bathing suits and ski undergarments.

sweater jersey knit
Smooth-faced knit with or without a design knitted in. Used for sport sweaters and many types of sports apparel.

terry cloth
Fabric with looped pile that may be woven or knitted, usually of cotton and cotton-blend fibers; frequently used for bathing-suit coverups, jogging wear, and tennis sportswear.

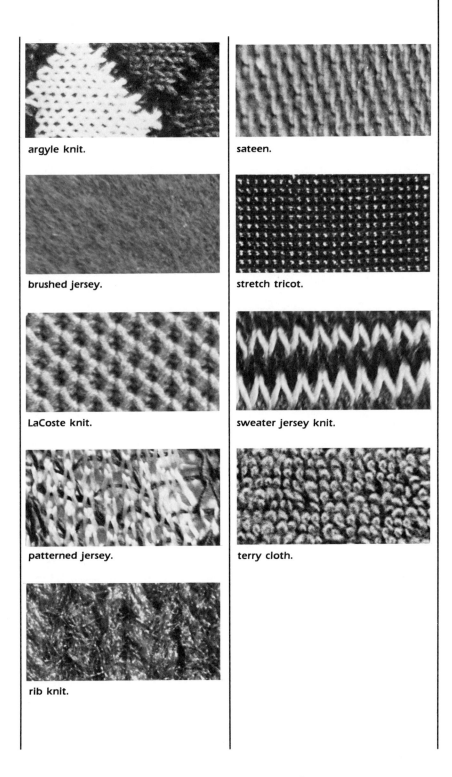

argyle knit.

sateen.

brushed jersey.

stretch tricot.

LaCoste knit.

sweater jersey knit.

patterned jersey.

terry cloth.

rib knit.

2

Above-
the-
Waist
Apparel

Blouses
Jackets
Shirts
Sweaters
Vests
Top-weight Fabrics

Blouses

Loose-fitting lightweight garment generally worn by women and children; covers neck to hip area of the body.

blouson
Any style blouse with fullness at the hip line or slightly above. Fullness is held with a drawstring or elastic. Usually worn over a skirt or pants. Fashionable in 1960s, late 1970s, and 1980s.

body blouse
Form-fitting blouse with pant section attached. Opening snaps together at crotch. Popular with women in 1960s, especially with miniskirts. Also called a body shirt.

bustier (boost-e-*ay*)
Strapless top, either held in place by an elasticized shirring or made of a stretchy, clinging knit. Also called tube top or "boob" tube. Fashionable in 1950s, late 1970s, and 1980s.

choli *or* cholee *or* coli
Rib-length blouse worn with sari by Indian women. Usually features scoop neckline and short set-in sleeves. Traditional part of Hindu women's costume; fashionable in United States in late 1960s.

cossack
Blouse with high stand-up collar, side closing, full sleeves, and embroidered band trim. Blouse originally worn by Russian cossacks (horsemen). Adapted for men and women; popular in the 1960s and 1970s, after release of the movie *Dr. Zhivago*. Also called Zhivago or Russian blouse.

Gibson waist
Tailored, high-neckline blouse with full leg-o'-mutton sleeves. First made famous by women whose portraits were painted by artist Charles Dana Gibson in the 1890s and early 1900s. Adaptations popular many times throughout the twentieth century.

gypsy
See *peasant blouse.*

halter
Backless blouse without sleeves, held at neck by buttons or ties. Popular for sunbathing and evening wear.

middy
Adapted from the shirt worn by United States Navy sailors. Front of collar forms a V; back collar is square. Collar trimmed with braid. Fashionable at various times in twentieth century for women and children. Frequently designed in red, white, and blue color combinations.

overblouse
Any style blouse worn outside skirt or pants by women and children. Fashionable in the 1960s.

peasant
Style adapted from European peasant groups; gathered at neckline and sleeve edge; frequently trimmed with embroidery and other rich trims. Also called gypsy blouse.

russian
See *cossack.*

sailor blouse
See *middy.*

shell
Plain, sleeveless blouse with jewel neckline worn by women; made of knitted or woven fabric; a classic style worn under suits from 1950 through 1980s or worn with coordinating skirts and pants.

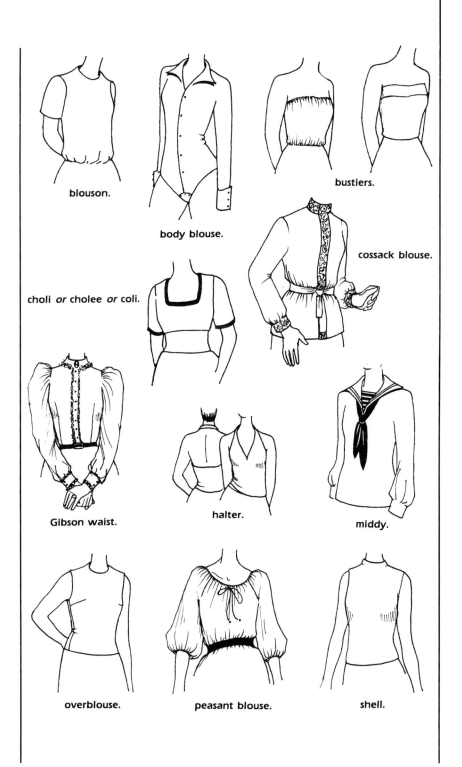

blouson.

body blouse.

bustiers.

cossack blouse.

choli *or* cholee *or* coli.

Gibson waist.

halter.

middy.

overblouse.

peasant blouse.

shell.

shirtwaist
Women's and girls' blouse styled similar to a man-tailored shirt. A classic style during twentieth century. Also called a tailored blouse.

slip-on
A pullover blouse of any style made without front or back closings.

smock
A full-cut blouse worn by men, women, and children as a coverup while easel painting or doing other types of crafts.

tailored *or* **man-tailored**
See *shirtwaist*.

tube top
See *bustier*.

tunic
Long, midthigh-length overblouse of any style. Worn by men over pants; worn by women over pants or skirts.

yoke
Contains a fitted portion over the neck and shoulder area and fullness in the body; worn by men, women, and children.

Zhivago
See *cossack*.

Jackets

Short outer garment with hemline between waist and hips; front opening. Worn by men, women, and children.

battle
Waist-length jacket with fitted waistband, breast pockets, and notched collar. Front closes with buttons or zippers. Adapted from the army jacket worn in World War II. Also called Eisenhower jacket.

bell boy
Fitted, waist-length jacket, with stand-up collar, trimmed with brass buttons; worn by messenger boys, hotel bellhops, and band members; adaptations worn by women and children.

blazer
A classic jacket worn by men, women, and children. Jacket features semifit, single-breasted opening with brass buttons, three patch pockets, notched collar, and embroidered emblem over breast pocket.

blouson (bloo-*sohn*)
Blousing at waistline or below is created with elastic or drawstring; used for men's, women's, and children's jackets.

bolero
Very short, above-the-waist jacket with round neckline, collarless and buttonless; frequently trimmed with embroidery and braid. Derived from the name of a Spanish dance. Worn mostly by women and children.

bomber
Adapted for men, women, and children from waist-length jacket worn by United States Air Force pilots. Usually made of leather with a

shirtwaist.

slip-on.

smock.

tunic.

yoke.

battle jacket.

bell boy.

blazer.

blouson jacket.

bolero.

bomber.

sheepskin or pile fabric lining. Oversized jackets fashionable for men and women in the 1980s.

box
Straight, unfitted jacket worn by women and children; fashionable in 1940s, 1950s, and 1970s for women.

bush
See *safari*.

cardigan
Collarless jacket with front button closing; classic style for women and children.

Chanel
A cardigan jacket made famous by designer Coco Chanel in the 1930s. Edge usually trimmed with braid. A classic style worn primarily by women.

dinner
Hip-length semiformal jacket worn by men. Collar can be shawl or tailored notch, sometimes faced with satin or velvet fabric. Also called tuxedo jacket.

Edwardian
Long-length, fitted jacket with deep back vents, double-breasted closure, and wide lapels; fashionable for men in the late 1960s.

Eisenhower
See *battle*.

Eton
Fitted, waist-length jacket with stand-up or wide notched collar; adapted from jackets worn by boys at Eton College, England. Worn by young boys, men, and women.

fly-away
Back and sides of jacket have an exaggerated flare; waist is usually fitted.

Fashionable for women's jackets in the 1980s.

hunting
See *Equestrian* and *Hunting Outfits, Section 1*.

leisure
Loose, box-style jacket worn by men with or without a belt; usually has a convertible collar shirt. Fashionable in the 1970s.

Lindbergh
See *windbreaker*.

lumber
Wool plaid jacket originally worn by lumber tradesmen, adapted for men, women, and children. Styles can be hip length or waist length.

mackinaw
Double-breasted, belted jacket usually made of heavy blanketlike wool fabric in plaid or stripe design. Adapted from the coats worn by men as they bartered with Indians at Fort Mackinac, Michigan. Used today by men, women, and children.

Mao
Named after Chinese leader Mao Tsetung. Has side front closing and stand up-collar; frequently used as a uniform jacket for doctors, dentists, and other medical-profession uniforms.

Nehru
Slim, hip-length, slightly fitted jacket with stand-up collar; adapted from coat worn by Jawaharlal Nehru, Indian prime minister from 1947 to 1964; fashionable for men in the early 1960s.

Norfolk
Box-pleat front with slot for matching belt; adapted from jacket worn by

box jacket.

cardigan.

Chanel jacket.

dinner jacket.

fly-away jacket.

leisure jacket.

Edwardian jacket.

lumber jackets.

Eton jacket.

character Dr. Watson of Sherlock Holmes stories. Worn by men, women, and children; fashionable in the 1960s for men and women.

parka
Hooded jacket made of windproof fabrics such as rip stop and others; sometimes quilted or lined in pile fabric. Used by men, women, and children.

pea
Double-breasted, hip-length jacket with large buttons and vertical slash pockets. Usually made of navy-blue blanket-type wool fabric; adapted from the United States Navy sailor coat uniform. Used by men, women, and children. Also called pea coat or pilot coat.

peplum
Jacket with separate section between waist and hipline. Section can be pleated or gathered to create flare. Fashionable in the 1970s and 1980s.

safari
Made of khaki cotton and worn originally for hunting trips in Africa. Single-breasted body, bellows pockets, and fabric belt. Worn by men, women, and children.

smoking
Buttonless wraparound jacket with soft fabric tie; usually made of velvet with satin shawl collar; worn for informal entertaining by men. Adaptations also worn by women in 1960s.

sport
Very similar to the blazer in styling; made without the emblem on breast pocket and with coordinating buttons rather than brass buttons; term used to describe jacket worn by men with contrasting pants.

tuxedo
See *dinner*.

Windbreaker
Trademark name for a lightweight waist-length jacket with zipper front; frequently made of nylon rip stop.

mackinaw.

Mao jacket.

Nehru jacket.

Norfolk jacket.

parka.

pea.

peplum.

safari.

smoking.

sport.

Windbreaker.

Shirts

Garment worn on upper part of body by men, women, and children. A variety of collars, necklines, and sleeves can be combined with many shirt bodies. Some are worn outside apparel below the waist and some are tucked inside pants or skirts.

athletic shirt
See *tank top.*

Ben Casey
An overshirt with straight body, stand-up collar, and shoulder-button closing. Commonly worn by medical professionals. Named after the title character of the *Ben Casey* television series of the 1960s.

body
Very close-fitting man's shirt. Fashionable in the 1960s and early 1970s. Women's version has pant section with snap crotch. See also *body blouse.*

button-down
See *collars; Ivy League* shirt.

Continental cut
See *European cut.*

cossack
See *cossack,* under *Blouse.*

cowboy
Styled from shirts worn by the American cowboy. Shirt body usually has front and back yoke, gripper closings instead of buttons, and piping trim. Some are decorated on the yoke with colorful embroidery. Fashionable in the late 1970s and early 1980s.

dashiki
Adapted from shirt often worn by African men. Usually collarless, with full body and full-flowing sleeves. Fashionable for both men and women in the late 1960s and early 1970s.

dress
Shirt usually worn by men under business suits or formal tuxedos. Body can be plain or ruffled. Collar usually has a band and is designed to accommodate a tie. A classic shirt for men.

European cut
Fitted shirt worn by men, usually as a dress shirt. Body tapered with waist darts. Also called Continental cut. Popular for men, especially young men, in the 1960s, 1970s, and 1980s.

football jersey
Adapted for children and teenagers from the uniform worn by football players. Pullover shirt is made of jersey knit cotton or cotton and polyester fibers. Round neckline made of contrasting rib knit; sleeves have contrasting color bands; number is sewn to front and back. Popular in 1960s and 1970s.

Guayabera (gwah-ya-*bare*-a)
Usually worn by men as a casual overshirt or lightweight jacket. Box-style shirt body has convertible collar and is sometimes decorated with embroidered front panels. Adapted from the shirt worn by guava-tree growers of Cuba. Fashionable for men in late 1970s and early 1980s.

Hawaiian
Boxy overshirt made of large floral print cotton, with front-button closing and convertible collar. Introduced for men in the 1940s. Fashionable for men, women, and children in the 1980s.

Henley
Collarless, short-sleeve, knitted pullover shirt with placket front; con-

Ben Casey shirt.

body shirt.

cowboy shirt.

dashiki.

dress shirt.

European-cut shirt.

football jersey.

Guayaberas.

Hawaiian shirt.

Henley shirt.

trasting rib knit used to trim front closing, sleeves, and hem. Worn as casual wear by men, women, and children.

Ivy League
Named after the shirts worn by men who attended the seven eastern Ivy League schools. Shirt has button-down or eyelet collar, back yoke with pleat, and is usually made of Oxford cloth or chambray. Popular for men, women, and children in 1950s and 1980s. Also called Oxford shirt.

overshirt
Any style shirt worn over pants, skirts, or shorts by men, women, or children. Popular classic for casual wear.

Oxford
See *Ivy League*.

polo
Knitted stripe or solid pullover shirt with crew neck or square collar. Classic sportswear shirt for men, women, and children.

ruffle
Dress shirt, the front of which is covered with ruffles. Usually worn by men under formal tuxedos.

sport
Colorful solid, print, or plaid shirt worn for informal occasions without a tie; usually worn by men and boys.

sweatshirt
Fleece-backed, cotton-knit pullover, with ribbed neck and wristbands. Worn by men, women, and children for exercise, jogging, or other sports and for many informal activities. During 1960s, 1970s, and 1980s, shirts often decorated with slang expressions, school names, or other wording.

tank top
Shirt worn by men and women for active sports and other informal occasions. Pullover shirt has scooped neckline and large sleeveless openings for arms. Also called athletic shirt.

Tom Jones
Full-body shirt with yoke, drop full sleeves, and ruffles held at wrist. Named after the shirts worn by Albert Finney in the 1965 movie *Tom Jones*. Fashionable for men and women in the 1960s and 1970s.

T-shirt
Knit pullover shirt usually made of cotton or cotton and polyester with ribbed round neck and short or long sleeves set into a wide armhole opening to form T shape. Worn by men, women, and children with slogans, names, or pictures printed on the front. Also worn by men as an undergarment. Very popular with teenagers during the 1960s and 1970s.

Ivy League shirt.

polo shirts.

overshirt.

sport shirt.

ruffle shirt.

sweatshirt.

tank top.

Tom Jones shirt.

T-shirt.

Sweaters

Classic garment made of knitted or crocheted fabrics. Fibers used include acrylic, polyester, cotton, wool, mohair, cashmere, and nylon. Styles may be sporty or elegant.

cardigan
Collarless button-down sweater usually worn over a shirt, blouse, or dress by men, women, and children. A classic style in the twentieth century.

coat
Bulky-knit sweater worn instead of a coat. Hemline may be at hip or below; may have collar or be collarless; usually buttons or ties at center front. Worn by men, women, and children.

crew or crew-neck
Round, rib-knit-neckline pullover sweater named after the sweaters worn by college rowing teams. Fashionable in the 1950s and 1980s.

fanny
Long sweater with wide rib knit band at buttocks or "fanny." Fashionable for women in the early 1970s, returned to fashion in 1980s.

fisherman's
Natural-color-wool, bulky hand knit made with cable stripe and seed stitches. Named fisherman because the pattern formed by the cables and stitches identified the name and village of the fisherman that wore it. If fisherman drowned and was later recovered, he could be identified by his sweater. Popular in the 1960s and 1980s.

intarsia
Design technique used on any sweater to impart a dressy look. The design is knitted into a solid color fabric. Fashionable for women in the late 1970s and early 1980s.

letter sweater
A heavy-knit cardigan or other sweater with patch pockets and appliqué letters and numbers on chest and sleeve. Usually worn by members of school sports teams. In the 1950s, it was fashionable for football and basketball players to give them to their favorite girl. Also called a varsity or school sweater.

pointelle
Any sweater knitted or crocheted with lacy ribs. Generally worn by women and girls for dressy occasions.

poor boy
Form-fitting rib-knit pullover with turtleneck or round neck and roll-up sleeves. Fashionable in the mid-1960s for men, women, and children.

pullover
Any sweater free of center, side, or back opening; it pulls over the head.

school sweater
See *letter sweater.*

shell
Collarless, sleeveless pullover with turtleneck, mock turtleneck, or round neckline; usually a solid color. Worn under a woman's suit instead of a blouse. Fashionable in the 1950s; since then, a classic for women.

shrink
Short, narrow, sleeveless pullover sweater worn by women and children. Usually crocheted with colorful wool yarns. A fad fashion for children and women in the early 1970s.

cardigan.

coat sweater.

crew sweater.

fisherman's sweater.

fanny sweater.

pointelle.

intarsia sweater.

letter sweater.

poor boy sweater.

pullover.

shell.

shrink sweater.

ski
Crew-neck pullover with designs knitted in the body and sleeves of the sweater. Usually worn for skiing or as informal attire during cold weather by men, women, and children.

varsity
See *letter sweater.*

Vests

Sleeveless garment worn by men, women, and children. The length is variably above the waist, at the waist, or below the waist. Vest may match or contrast with apparel worn below the waist. Also called waistcoat, weskit, or vestee.

bolero
Above-the-waist vest worn by women and children; often the neckline and front are trimmed with braid. A classic fashion, but very popular in the mid-1970s and early 1980s.

doublet
Form-fitting vest, sleeveless or having a slight cap sleeve, that usually laces up the front. Frequently made of leather. Originally worn by men in the fifteenth century; today worn by men, women, and children.

fisherman
Waist-length vest used by fishermen and other sportsmen; contains many pockets for fishing or other sports gear.

formal
Single- or double-breasted vest made to match or coordinate with men's formal suits.

jerkin
Sleeveless waist-length or just-below-waist vest worn by men, women, and children. Derived from a garment worn by men from the fifteenth through the seventeenth centuries.

Pakistani
Very short vest similar to a bolero; richly decorated with braid, embroidery, and tassels, and fastened in front with invisible hooks. Fashionable in the late 1960s and early 1970s as part

ski sweater.

bolero.

doublet.

fisherman's vest.

formal vests.

jerkin.

Pakistani vest.

of the ethnic look for women and children.

sweater
Sleeveless knitted vest worn to the waist or slightly below by men, women, and children. A classic garment.

tabard
Long, loose, rectangular pieces of fabric joined at sides with ties or fabric tabs. Fashionable for women in the 1970s. Adapted from garments worn by knights from the thirteenth through the sixteenth centuries.

vestee
See *weskit*.

veston
See *weskit*.

waistcoat
See *weskit*.

weskit
Another name for vest or very fitted, sleeveless, collarless, vest that buttons at center front; has pointed edges at hem and welt pockets at waistline. Worn by men, women, and children as a classic fashion, particularly under suits. Very fashionable in the 1970s for women and in the 1970s and 1980s for men. Also called waistcoat, veston, vestee.

Top-weight Fabrics

batiste
Cotton or cotton-blend woven fabric with sheer, lightweight texture; used for blouses and dresses.

broadcloth
Firmly woven, lightweight, plain weave with a slight crosswise rib. Commonly made of cotton, cotton blends, or wool.

calico
Plain weave, lightweight fabric printed with small floral design. Usually made of cotton or cotton-blend fibers.

chambray
Lightweight plain weave made with colored warp yarns and white filling yarns. Usually made of cotton or cotton-blend fibers.

chiffon
Soft, sheer, smooth plain weave. Frequently made of silk, polyester, rayon, or nylon fibers.

crepe
Pebbly or crinkled-surface fabric created from high-twist yarns, from an irregular weave, or with chemicals. Made of many fibers.

crepe de chine
Crepe fabric with a low-luster surface.

dimity
Cotton or cotton-blend sheer lightweight fabric made with lengthwise cords.

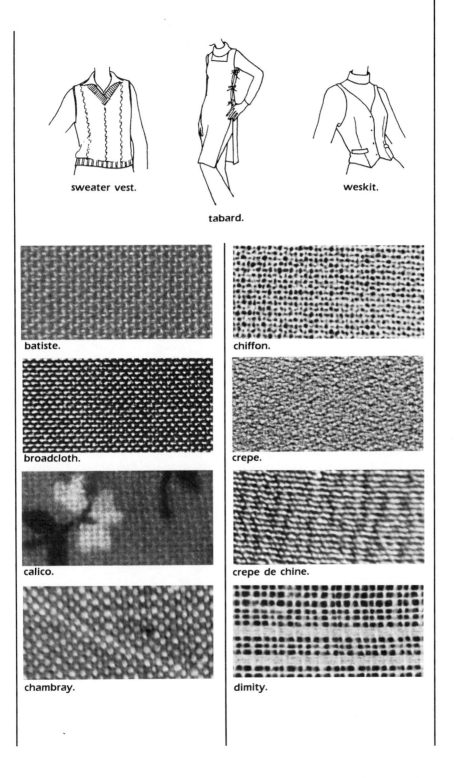

sweater vest.

tabard.

weskit.

batiste.

chiffon.

broadcloth.

crepe.

calico.

crepe de chine.

chambray.

dimity.

dotted Swiss
Fine lightweight sheer fabric with dotted areas woven or flocked on. Usually made of cotton or cotton-blend fibers.

foulard
Small overall print used on soft, lightweight, twill-weave fabric. Made with smooth filament yarn of silk or synthetic fibers.

gauze
Very loosely woven plain weave generally made of cotton or cotton-blend fibers.

georgette
Very loosely woven sheer fabric with pebbly surface. Usually made of silk or the synthetic fibers: polyester, rayon, nylon.

gingham
Lightweight plain weave of two-color check made from cotton, cotton blends, or synthetic fibers.

honan
Lightweight plain weave with slightly uneven surface created from thick and thin yarns. Frequently made of silk or from synthetic, silk-lookalike fibers.

interlock knit
Fine rib knit with smooth face. Generally made of synthetic fibers.

lawn
Slightly stiff, fine, lightweight plain weave fabric. Generally made of cotton or cotton blends.

matelasse
Puffy design, created from a medium- to heavy-weight double-cloth weave. Frequently made of silk or synthetic silk-lookalike fibers.

organdy
Lightweight, sheer, stiff, plain-weave fabric made of cotton or cotton blends.

organza
Similar to organdy but has a low luster because it is made of filament yarns of silk or man-made fibers.

oxford
Soft, lightweight, basket-weave fabric. Generally made of cotton or cotton-blend fibers.

dotted Swiss.

interlock knit.

foulard.

lawn.

gauze.

matelasse.

georgette.

organdy.

gingham.

organza.

honan.

oxford.

percale
Very fine cotton or cotton-blend yarn used in a lightweight plain weave; frequently printed.

piqué (pee-*kay*)
Raised, textured design created from a dobby (small geometric design) weave. Fabric is crisp, medium weight, and usually made of cotton or cotton-blend fibers.

plissé
Puckered surface created by a finish used on a plain weave, lightweight cotton or cotton-blend fabric.

seersucker
Permanet puckered stripe created by a novelty weave. Fabric is lightweight and usually made of cotton or cotton-blend fibers.

single-knit jersey
Smooth-knitted fabric created by knit stitches on the face and purl stitches on the reverse side. Any fiber can be used.

surah
Lustrous, lightweight fabric made of very fine twill weave. Usually made of silk or silklike synthetic fibers, and frequently printed.

voile
Sheer, crisp, lightweight plain weave with high-twist spun yarns of cotton or cotton-blend fibers. Slightly more sheer than lawn fabric.

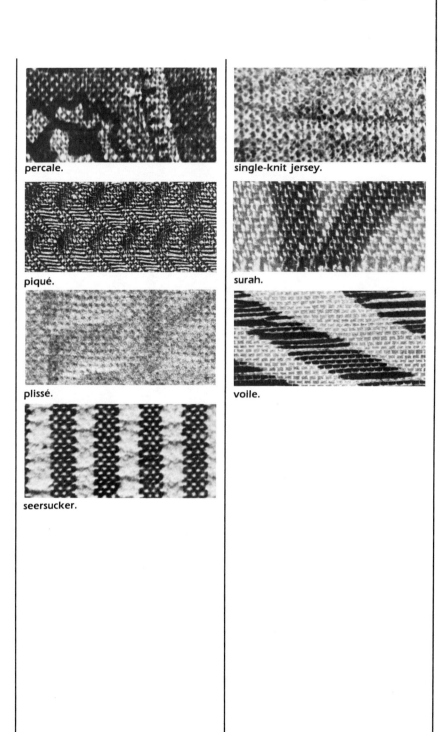

percale.

single-knit jersey.

piqué.

surah.

plissé.

voile.

seersucker.

3

Below-the-Waist Apparel

Skirts
Pants
Bottom-weight Fabrics

Skirts

Free-hanging part of an outer or undergarment covering the body from waist down. Types include:

apron
See *tunic.*

balloon
Fitted at the waistline with fullness held in a fitted band at hemline.

bell
Gathered or pleated at waistline and stiffened to form bell shape.

bias gored
Sectioned skirt with fabric sections cut on the diagonal; popular fabrics include tartan and tattersall plaids or stripes.

broomstick
Straight, full skirt pleated by wetting and drying around a broomstick.

bubble
Similar to balloon but has more fullness at waistline; also called tulip skirt.

circular
Created from a full, half, or quarter circle of fabric.

culotte
A divided skirt with leg sections; also called gauchos, divided skirt, pants skirt, or split skirt.

dirndl
Straight skirt gathered at waist.

divided
See *culotte.*

dome
Similar to bell but with more exaggerated fullness at the hipline.

draped
See *sarong.*

flared
Fits flat over waistline area and full at hemline.

full
A gathered, pleated, or flared skirt with greatest fullness at hemline; often called peasant or gypsy skirt.

gaucho
See *culotte.*

golf
Cut with ease of movement in mind, either flared or culotte type, often without waistband and usually with a pocket.

gored
Sectioned skirt. Some designs are flat at the waist and wide at the hemline; other designs have soft gathers or pleats at the waistline; may have two, three, four, or more sections.

gypsy
See *full.*

handkerchief
Uneven skirt lengths with pointed edges as in a handkerchief; usually created in lightweight, see-through fabric; popular in 1920s, 1960s, and 1970s.

bias-gored skirt.

balloon skirt.

bell skirt.

broomstick skirt.

bubble skirt.

circular skirt.

culotte.

dirndl skirt.

dome skirt.

flared skirt.

full skirt.

handkerchief skirt.

golf skirts.

gored skirts.

harem
Gathered at waistline and held to lining at hemline; patterned after court costumes of Near East; same design principles applied to design of pants.

hip hugger
Any skirt that rides low on the hips, below the natural waistline; fashionable during the 1960s.

hoop
Full skirt held out with wire hoops or crinolines.

hula
Grass skirt worn by Hawaiian women.

kilt
Knife-pleated short skirt that wraps to one side and is held closed with leather straps, buckles, or decorative pins; patterned after tartan wool skirt worn by Scottish men as part of national dress.

morning glory
Gored skirt with flare at the bottom, shaped like the flower of the same name. Also called trumpet.

overskirt
Separate skirt worn over another as in gypsy or peasant costume.

peasant
See *full.*

peg-top
Pleated at waist and hips and very tapered at hemline; also called pegged skirt.

pleated
A fold of fabric done in one of the following ways:

accordian pleat Narrow, pressed in, or edge stitched; also called crystal pleat.

box pleat Double pleat formed by folds that go in opposite directions.

inverted pleat Folds face each other; can be stitched or left free.

kick pleat An inverted or knife pleat stitched closed from waistline to within 7 or 8 inches of hemline. Open pleat portion allows for walking ease.

knife pleat Narrow folds that face one direction.

ruffled
Hemline of skirt finished with fullness greater than body of skirt.

sarong
Wrapped skirt with gathers or soft drape at waist and hip line; fitted close to leg at hemline; also called draped skirt.

scooter
Very short culotte with panel over front and back; also called skort.

harem skirt.

hip hugger.

hoop skirt.

hula skirt.

kilt.

morning glory skirt.

overskirt.

peg-top skirt.

accordion pleat skirt.

box pleat skirt.

inverted pleat skirt.

kick pleat skirt.

knife pleat skirt.

ruffled skirt.

sarong.

scooter skirt.

sheath
See *straight*.

slit
Narrow, fitted skirt with openings at side, front, or back to allow movement; sometimes slits are thigh high as in late 1970s; also called tapered.

split
See *culotte*.

straight
Fitted, slim, often called a sheath or tapered skirt.

swing
Flared skirt with many gores; popular in late 1930s and often since.

tapered skirt
See *straight* or *slit*.

tiered
See *tunic*.

trumpet gore
See *morning glory*.

tulip
See *bubble* skirt.

tunic
An overskirt shorter than the skirt it covers; often called tiered skirt or apron.

wrap
Two free edges wrap around body and are held at waist with ties, buttons, snaps, or hooks; opening can be at front, back, or sides.

yoke
Skirt with separate fitted section from waist to hipline; fashionable in the 1950s and in early 1980s.

skirt lengths

ballerina See *midi*.

cocktail See *street*.

formal See *maxi*.

granny See *maxi*.

long See *maxi*.

maxi Hemline at ankle or just covering instep; fashionable in late 1960s and early 1970s; also called long, granny, or formal length.

micro-mini Just covers thighs; popular in 1960s, revived in 1980s.

midi Hemline midcalf; faddish name in late 1960s and early 1970s. Also called ballerina length and longuette.

mini Usually a flared skirt; hemline 4 to 6 inches above knee; popular in 1960s, revived in 1980s.

street-length Hemline 1 to 3 inches below knee. Fashionable in early 1940s, early 1960s, and 1980s. Called cocktail length in evening wear.

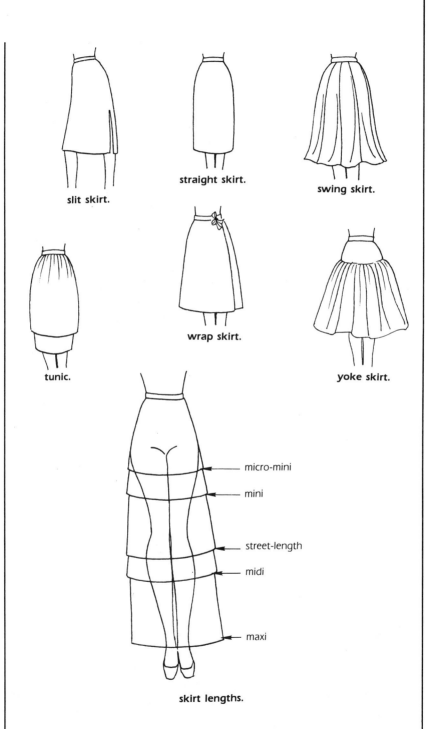

slit skirt.

straight skirt.

swing skirt.

tunic.

wrap skirt.

yoke skirt.

micro-mini

mini

street-length

midi

maxi

skirt lengths.

Pants

An outer garment that covers each leg separately, generally from the waist down; also called trousers or slacks; worn by men, women, and children during the twentieth century.

ankle
Slim-legged pant hemmed at ankle; popular term in 1980s.

baggies
Wide at hip and narrow at ankle. Width at hip frequently achieved by waist tucks; popular in 1980s.

bell bottoms
Legs flare from knee to hemline to give a bell shape; adapted from the pants worn by sailors; fashionable for youth in 1960s and 1970s; also called flare legs.

Bermuda
Short pant that ends just above the knee and fits close to the leg; worn by men on the island of Bermuda; adapted in the United States for men and women as a classic fashion; also called walking or, when cuffed at hem, a safari short.

bib
Pants with square, rectangle, or other shape attached at waist and usually having shoulder straps. A classic playwear item for children. Also called overalls or painter's pants.

bib-top pants
See *suspenders*.

blouson
Jumpsuit with blousy top. Popular in the 1970s for women and children.

blue jeans
See *jeans*.

boy short
Square leg hemmed 1 to 1½ inches below crotch; also called short short and hot pants in the early 1970s.

Capri
Very tapered legged pant that ends several inches above the ankle; popular during the 1950s, late 1970s and early 1980s.

clam digger
Midcalf-length pant styled generally with a full leg and cuffed; popular sportswear of 1950s and early 1980s.

classic pants
See *patio pants*.

Continental cut
Term given to shape of men's pants during 1950s; slim leg tapered to cuffless bottom; slit or welt pocket featured at the hip.

coveralls
See *fatigues*.

crawlers
Infants' or toddlers' long pants with bib and suspender straps; frequently made with snaps in legs.

culotte
See *culotte*, under *Skirts*.

deck
Fitted pant with hemline just below the knee; very fashionable for boatwear in 1950s and 1960s; today a classic sportswear item.

dungarees
See *jeans*.

elephant bells
Similar to bell bottoms but with exaggerated flare from knee to hemline; hem usually covers the shoe; a "hippie" trademark during 1960s.

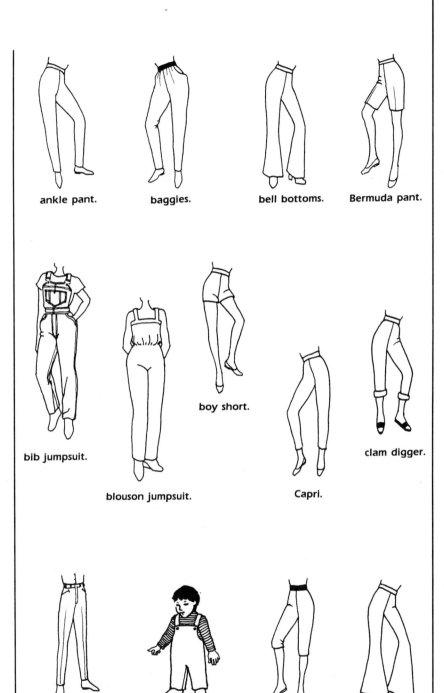

ankle pant.

baggies.

bell bottoms.

Bermuda pant.

bib jumpsuit.

blouson jumpsuit.

boy short.

Capri.

clam digger.

Continental-cut pant.

crawlers.

deck pant.

elephant bells.

fatigues
Name given to pants worn by United States Army men and women; sometimes name given to coveralls worn by same. Generally made of denim or other sturdy fabric, in olive drab or camouflage colors. Frequently used today as a coverup or uniform for sky divers, mechanics, astronauts, and race-car drivers. Also called coveralls.

flare leg
See *bell bottoms.*

gaucho
See *culotte*, under *Skirts.*

harem
Very full pants gathered at waist and ankle; soft and fluid lines; popular as lounge wear; important fashion influence of early 1980s.

hip huggers
Usually long pants with waistline at hipline; popular during middle and late 1960s.

hot pants
See *boy short.*

Jamaica short
Midthigh-length short with hemline in-between Bermuda and short short or boy short; derived from shorts worn at the island resorts of Jamaica.

jeans
Originally derived from work pants made of denim fabric named "jean"; today, name given to pants with pockets on front and back that usually have decorative stitching; other names include: dungarees, Levi's, overalls, and blue jeans.

jodhpurs
See *equestrian outfits Active Sportswear, Section 1.*

jogging
See *jogging outfits, Active Sportswear, Section 1.*

knickers
Knee-length pants with full cut gathered into a band. Worn by boys in 1920s and 1930s; fashionable for women in 1970s and 1980s; also called knickerbockers.

Levi's
See *jeans.*

overalls
See *jeans; suspenders.*

painter's pants
See *suspenders.*

palazzo pants
Women's long-length pants with very wide flares from hipline to hemline; often created for lounging or evening attire.

patio pants
Ladies' classic pant with hemline ending at top of shoe; usually a natural-width leg; also called classic pant.

pedal pushers
Midcalf length women's pants fashionable in the late 1940s and 1950s; revived in the 1980s.

peg leg
Pleated or gathered top pant with very narrow width leg at hem; popular during 1950s, late 1970s, and early 1980s.

petal pants
Slim-legged pant with wraparound overskirt shaped similar to a flower petal.

pull-on
Any leg-style pant with completely elasticized waistline.

fatigues.

harem pant.

hip huggers.

Jamaica short.

jeans.

knickers.

palazzo pants.

patio pants.

pedal pushers.

peg leg pant.

petal pants.

pull-on pant.

romper
Blousy top and short pants in combination. Worn by women and children. Popular in the 1970s.

safari short
See *Bermuda short.*

sailor pants
Uniform pant of men in the United States Navy; features a double-button front opening, lacing at back waist, and wide flare leg; adaptations called bell bottoms.

short short
See *boy short.*

ski pant
See *skiwear,* Section 1.

straight legs
Slim-legged pant; width of leg less than 18 inches wide. Fashionable in the late 1970s and early 1980s; in the 1960s called stovepipe.

strapless
Pants attached to tube top. Generally worn by women for evening wear. Popular in the 1970s.

surfers
Tight-fitting pant ending at the knee; popular in the 1960s; originated with California surfers.

suspender
Wide-leg pant with straps hooked to a front bib; frequently made of denim or other sturdy fabric; worn as a uniform by farmers, painters, and carpenters; also called overalls, painter's pants, and bib-top pants.

Sweat
See *jogging outfits, Section 1.*

Tailored
Tailored blouse attached to pants. Worn by women and children for day or evening wear. Fashionable in the 1970s.

Tennis shorts
See *tennis outfits, Section 1.*

toreador
Tight-fitting pants hemmed just below the knee; waistline is wide and generally features braid trim like that worn by the Spanish bullfighter; fashionable in the late 1950s, early 1960s, and 1980s.

walking short
See *Bermuda short.*

zippered pant
Any pant that opens with zipper at waistline; used in men's, women's, and children's pants in 1970s and 1980s; zipper commonly located at front seam; front zipper called fly front.

Zouave (zoo-*of*)
Full pant gathered or pleated at waistline and hemline; usually knee or below-knee length; patterned from the French soldier's (called Zouave) uniform; fashionable for women in the 1980s.

romper.

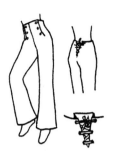

sailor pants.

straight legs.

strapless jumpsuit.

surfers.

suspender pant.

tailored jumpsuit.

toreador pants.

zippered pant.

Zouave pant.

Bottom-weight Fabrics

bengaline
Lustrous fabric with prominent crosswise ribs, made of wool, cotton, rayon, silk, or synthetic fibers.

brocade
Luxurious fabric made on a Jacquard loom; the pattern usually includes a slightly raised design created by a combination of satin, rib, plain, or twill weaves.

chino
A firm twill-weave fabric with low luster; pants with "jean" styling made of this fabric are called chinos; frequently made of polyester and cotton fibers or 100 percent cotton.

corduroy
Constructed of lengthwise, filling, cut-pile ribs (called wales); wales may vary in width from fine pinwales to wide-wales; cotton or cotton and polyester are fibers most frequently used.

crash
Coarse-textured, plain-weave fabric of medium weight; made from linen, cotton, and rayon fibers.

denim
Medium- to heavy-weight fabric constructed in twill weave with colored warp yarns, usually of indigo-blue dye and filling yarns of white or gray; indigo-blue dye fades when washed; one of the most popular fabrics for jeans during 1950s, 1960s, and 1970s; denim name originated from Nîmes, France, where the fabric was first made; commonly made of cotton or cotton and polyester fibers.

duck
A plain weave, medium- to heavy-weight fabric made of cotton or cotton and polyester fibers; resembles canvas and sailcloth; canvas is heavier whereas sailcloth is lighter in weight.

faille
Distinguished by prominent crosswise ribs and a medium luster; fibers used include 100 percent silk or blends with rayon, polyester, nylon, and cotton.

flannel
Soft, light- to medium-weight fabric with brushed surface; woven with plain or twill weave using wool, cotton, and/or synthetic blend fibers.

gabardine
A durable medium-weight fabric constructed of the twill weave using wool, cotton, and polyester fibers. Diagonal ribs can be slight or pronounced depending on types of yarns used.

herringbone
Medium-weight fabric distinguished by rows of diagonals slanting away from each other; wool fiber is frequently used, but can also be made of cotton, polyester, acrylic, or a blend of these.

homespun
Medium-weight, loosely woven fabric with a coarse, uneven texture; fibers used include wool, rayon, cotton, and polyester or blends.

bengaline.

duck.

brocade.

faille.

chino.

flannel.

corduroy.

gabardine.

crash.

herringbone.

denim.

homespun.

houndstooth check
Irregularly shaped squares created by a variation of the twill weave. Usually two or more colors.

panne (*pan*) velvet
Fabric with pile pressed in one direction for a mirrorlike effect.

peau de soie (poe di *swa*)
Low-luster, satin-weave fabric with very fine ribbed effect; usually made of silk fiber or synthetics made to look like silk.

plaid
Any fabric woven with crossbars of different-colored yarns; most common types include:

tartan Combinations of various widths and colors that cross at right angles and form distinctive patterns; originally, the color patterns identified specific Scottish clans.

window-pane Widely spaced vertical and horizontal crossbars with one or two colors used.

ponte di Roma
A one-color double knit with fine, barely noticeable rib and a smooth face.

poplin
A durable, medium-weight, plain-weave fabric with fine horizontal ribs; commonly made of cotton or cotton and man-made fiber blends.

sateen
Low-luster fabric made of satin weave; generally made of cotton or cotton and polyester blends; the spun yarns give it a softer and fuzzier texture than satin.

satin
Lustrous fabric made of satin weave with filament yarns; face very smooth and back dull and rougher; frequently made of silk or man-made fibers that imitate the look of silk.

serge
Worsted yarns used in a twill weave to produce a heavy, durable, smooth-surface fabric; generally made of 100 percent wool or wool and synthetic blend fibers.

shantung
A plain-weave fabric, medium weight, with noticeable slub yarns; originally made from silk, but many man-made fibers are used today.

sharkskin
Medium-weight, twill-weave, semi-lustrous fabric; surface resembles the skin of a shark; usually made of worsted wool, silk, or synthetics made to look like wool and silk.

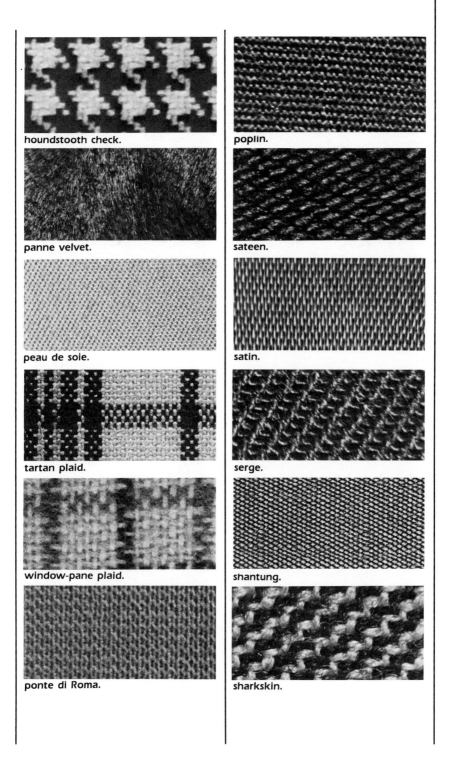

houndstooth check.

poplin.

panne velvet.

sateen.

peau de soie.

satin.

tartan plaid.

serge.

window-pane plaid.

shantung.

ponte di Roma.

sharkskin.

taffeta

Lustrous, stiff, plain-weave fabric made with filament yarns and heavier filling yarns to give slight crosswise rib; can be made of a variety of fibers but frequently silk, rayon, acetate, and nylon are used.

tweed

Medium- to heavy-weight fabric with a nubby, rough texture created with coarse woolen yarns; generally made of wool, man-made fibers, or both.

velour

Cut-pile fabric that can be woven or knitted but has more pile depth than velvet or velveteen; many fibers are used.

velvet

Warp-cut pile woven fabric made of filament yarns of silk, rayon, nylon or polyester fibers.

velveteen

A filling-pile woven fabric made of spun yarns of cotton fibers or man-made fibers made to look like cotton; pile is shorter than velvet.

whipcord

A heavy fabric with prominent round, diagonal twill lines; looks similar to gabardine but has more pronounced twill; commonly made of cotton, wool, or synthetic fibers.

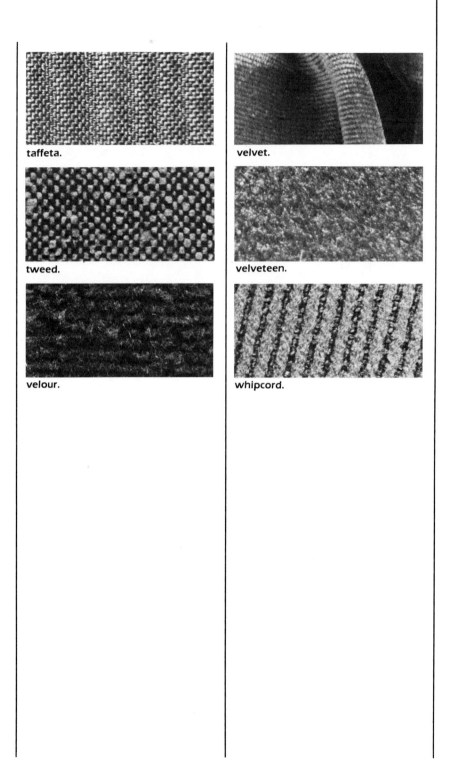

taffeta.

velvet.

tweed.

velveteen.

velour.

whipcord.

4

Accessories

Belts
Boots
Shoes
Slippers
Gloves
Hairstyles
Wigs
Hand Accessories
Handbags
Hats
Hosiery
Jewelry
Neckwear
Accessory Fabrics
and Materials

Belts

body chain
Chain of links arranged in a decorative way around the body; usually hooked together at waistline. Popular in the late 1960s.

chain
Metal or plastic links hooked together around the waistline.

cinch
Tight-fitting, elasticized belt of fabric, metal, or elastic; with clasp in front; popular during 1950s and 1970s. Can be wide or narrow.

cowboy
Wide hip belt, decorated with tooled design or studs, with gun holster attached. Adaptations omit holster. Popular in late 1970s.

cummerbund
Women's: soft, shirred fabric belt worn over a dress or a skirt.

Men's: wide, front-pleated fabric belt with a smooth fabric back. Shaped wide in front, narrow in back. Usually worn with formal attire.

garter
See *garter belt*, Section 9.

judo
Long tie belt worn with judo *gi* (uniform) and usually made of heavyweight twill tape. The color indicates achievement level: black is the highest; brown is intermediate; and white is for the novice. Other colors denote varying ranks. Sometimes called an obi belt.

macramé
Wide or narrow belt made by a series of hand knots. Can tie or buckle; tie type frequently beaded.

monk's
Rope tied around waist. Made of twisted rayon or cotton fibers and finished with tassels or knots at the end.

obi (o-bee)
A wide band worn high under the bosom and tied with narrow cord. Used on the kimono by Japanese women. Adaptations popular during the 1970s and 1980s.

sash
Soft belt that ties in bow or knot. Frequently used on women's and girls' dresses.

suspenders
Straps attached to a separate waistband or the waistband of the garment. Worn by men, women, and children.

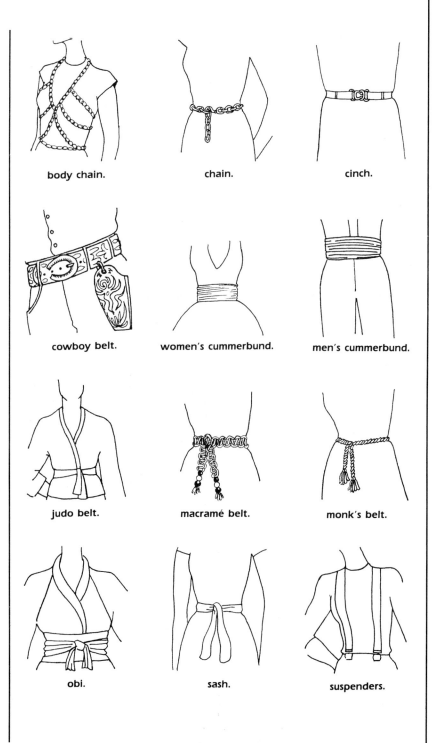

body chain.

chain.

cinch.

cowboy belt.

women's cummerbund.

men's cummerbund.

judo belt.

macramé belt.

monk's belt.

obi.

sash.

suspenders.

Boots

Protective footwear that extends to ankle or above. Can be worn in place of a shoe or over a shoe.

cavalier
Soft, ankle-high boot with a turned back cuff; made of a soft, pliable leather; generally worn by men.

chukka (*sha*-ka)
Soft ankle-high boot with short eyelet lacing and cushioned sole; frequently made of suede leather. Also called a desert boot.

construction
See *work boot.*

cowboy
Tooled design decorates a midcalf boot patterned from boots worn by the American cowboy; features pointed toe and stacked heel.

demi-boot
Dress boot that ends at the ankle.

desert
See *chukka.*

dress
Women's: midcalf to midthigh high; designed with the fashionable heel of the period.
  Men's: ankle high, smooth leather, plain front.

go-go boot
White midcalf boot with or without open toe; fashionable for women in the 1960s.

hiking boot
Sturdy lace-up boot worn for hiking.

jodhpur (*jod*-per)
Ankle-high boot buckled at one side of ankle; worn for horseback riding.

riding boot
Smooth top-grain leather knee-high boot; generally worn with jodhpur pants for horseback riding.

ski boot
Thick-soled, ankle-high boot; generally made of weatherproof leather, plastic, or other materials. Buckles and straps are used as fasteners.

work boot
Ankle-high lace-up boot made of tough-grade leather; usually thick soled. Also called construction boot.

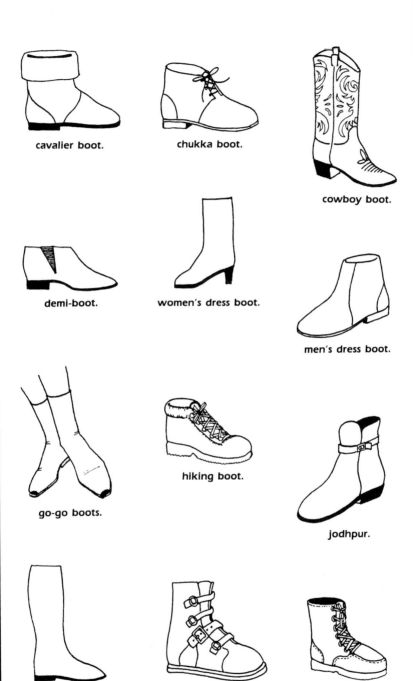

cavalier boot.

chukka boot.

cowboy boot.

demi-boot.

women's dress boot.

men's dress boot.

go-go boots.

hiking boot.

jodhpur.

riding boot.

ski boot.

work boot.

Shoes

Outer covering for feet; generally made of leather, vinyl, canvas, or straw. Types include:

ballerina slipper
See *ballet slipper,* under *Slipper.*

clog
See *sabot.*

espadrille
Slip-on shoe with canvas upper and rope-covered sole and heel.

loafer
Slip-on shoe with many style variations; low heel used. Types include:

deck shoe Slip-on with decorative leather tie; has rubber sole to prevent slipping on boat deck; also called boat shoe, topsider, or campus moccasin.

penny loafer Leather strip added at instep to hold coin; a classic school shoe popular in 1950s, 1970s, and 1980s.

tassel shoe Classic man's shoe; tassel attached at instep.

Mary Jane
Low-heel, rounded-top shoe with single strap across instep; usually made of patent leather; popular dress-up shoe for little girls.

moccasin
Slip-on shoe formed from a soft piece of leather; style worn by American Indian had only leather upper, no heel or sole.

monk strap
Plain vamp, low-heeled shoe with strap at instep.

mule
Open back, slide-on shoes; can be open or closed toe; also called slides or scuffs.

oxford
Low-cut shoe that laces at instep. Varieties include:

bal *or* balmoral Oxford with separate tongue stitched to the vamp.

blucher Vamp and tongue cut as one piece; quarters overlap vamp.

brogue Heavy-looking, generally worn by men, with decorative stitching or perforations; pointed toe designs called wing tips.

earth shoe Popular casual shoe of the 1970s and 1980s; one-piece sole and heel designed for walking comfort.

ghillie Women's oxford that laces through loops rather than eyelets; frequently has no tongue; vamp generally plain.

saddle shoe Lace-up shoe with contrasting sections; worn by men, women, and children; fashionable in 1970s and 1980s for schoolchildren.

sneaker Sports lace-up shoe made of canvas or materials that look like canvas, and rubber soles; worn by men, women, and children; other names include tennis, jogging, or sports shoe.

pump
Classic women's shoe with closed toe; a wide variety of heels and other style changes. Types include:

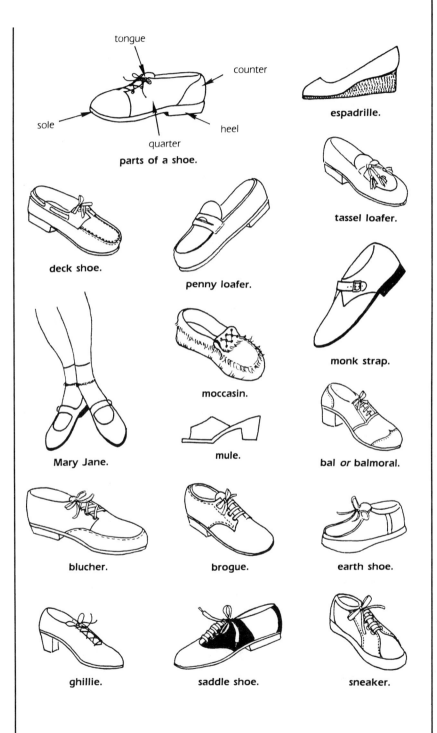

tongue

counter

sole

heel

quarter

parts of a shoe.

espadrille.

deck shoe.

penny loafer.

tassel loafer.

Mary Jane.

moccasin.

mule.

monk strap.

bal *or* **balmoral.**

blucher.

brogue.

earth shoe.

ghillie.

saddle shoe.

sneaker.

D'Orsay Closed toe and heel; low cut at back.

opera Closed plain vamp and closed heel.

platform Pump with thick sole.

sling-back Open-back pump held with strap at back.

spectator Vamp and counter constructed of constrasting color from rest of shoe upper.

T-strap Closed toe and heel; T-shaped strap holds foot at instep.

sabot
Sport shoe with thick soles made of wood or cork; shoe upper generally made of leather; also called clogs.

sandal
Open shoe held on foot with one or more straps. Varieties include:

ankle-wrap Straps tie around ankle.

exercise Wooden sole and heel molded to shape of foot; leather strap holds foot at instep, popular for women and children in the 1970s.

fisherman Low-heeled shoe with closed counter and woven leather straps across vamp; popular for men, women and children in 1970s and 1980s.

flip-flop See *thong*.

huarache (ha-*rah*-che) Sandal or pump made of woven or braided leather strips.

thong One strap between big and second toe; may or may not have heel strap; called flip-flops without heel strap, when made of rubber. Popular for men, women, and children, particularly as beach wear.

T-strap Open toe and open heel; strap in form of T holds shoe on the foot.

scuff
See *mule*.

slide
See *mule*.

shoe heels
The back, bottom part of a shoe. Types include:

boulevard Sturdy high heel; same width top and bottom.

cone Wide at top; narrow at bottom; fashionable for women in 1980s.

Continental High heel used on women's shoes; wide at top and narrow at bottom.

Cuban Medium to high heel with slight back curve; used on women's shoes in the 1940s and 1970s; lower version called military level.

demi wedge Combination of wedge and another shape heel such as Cuban.

donat Wedge with hole inside; frequently used on women's and children's shoes in late 1970s and the 1980s.

flat Low heel used on men's, women's, and children's shoes.

French Women's high heel, wide at top, narrow at bottom.

Louis XV Women's heel that curves inward at center and outward at top and bottom.

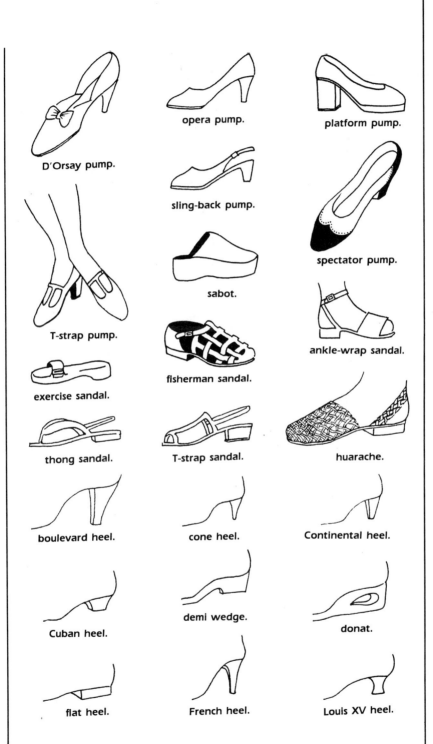

D'Orsay pump.

opera pump.

platform pump.

sling-back pump.

spectator pump.

sabot.

T-strap pump.

ankle-wrap sandal.

exercise sandal.

fisherman sandal.

thong sandal.

T-strap sandal.

huarache.

boulevard heel.

cone heel.

Continental heel.

Cuban heel.

demi wedge.

donat.

flat heel.

French heel.

Louis XV heel.

military See *Cuban heel.*

stacked Cuban or military heel made of horizontal layers of leather, wood, or simulated materials.

stiletto Women's high heel with very small base; steel rod through center; popular in 1950s, 1960s, and 1980s.

wedge Triangular base used on women's and children's shoes; popular in 1970s and 1980s.

wing-tip See *brogue.*

Slippers

Soft, usually low-heeled foot covering, worn indoors; types include:

ballet
Fabric or soft-kid foot covering with no heel and a flat sole; kid worn by dancers, fabric modifications worn by women and children.

bootee
Knitted foot covering worn by infants, or soft knitted slipper and sock worn by adults.

opera
Slipper covers front and back of foot; low cut at sides; flat heel for men; high heel for women called D'Orsay.

Romeo
Bootlike slipper worn by men; elastic insets at sides.

scuff
Soft, heelless, backless slipper worn by men, women, and children; usually toeless; frequently made of terry cloth, nylon tricot, or fur fabrics.

stacked heel.

stiletto heel.

wedge heel.

ballet slipper.

bootee.

opera slipper.

Romeo slipper.

scuff slipper.

Gloves

A covering for the hand that has separate sections for the fingers and thumb. Lengths are measured by buttons. A button represents 1 inch. The measurement begins just below the thumb and ends at arm's edge.

gauntlet
Wide flare above the wrist; worn with sportswear or western wear.

Isotoner
Trade name for very tight fitting glove with elasticized inserts; designed to massage the muscles in the fingers and hand.

mitt
Long, fingerless glove; generally worn with formal attire.

mitten
One section for the longer fingers and one for the thumb; generally worn with sportswear or children's outerwear for warmth.

mousquetaire (mos-keh-*tare*)
Long glove with slit and buttons at wrist; can be worn long on the arm or crushed down to wrist; used primarily for formal occasions.

shorty
Glove that ends at wrist or slightly above.

slip-on
Glove that slides over the hand without fasteners or openings.

glove parts
The pieces sewn together to make a glove. Parts include:

bolton thumb
Thumb is cut as part of body of glove; allows for thumb freedom.

fourchette (four-*shet*)
Inserts sewn between the fingers to give a very fitted shape.

French thumb
See *quirk thumb*.

quirk thumb
Also called a French thumb; sewn like a set-in thumb but contains a separate triangular section for greater thumb movement.

set-in thumb
Thumb is cut in one piece with elongated shape attached to glove body; used primarily on dress gloves.

glove seam types
Various methods are used to join glove parts. Seam types include:

inseam
Two edges are sewn right sides together.

outseam
Two edges sewn wrong sides together; commonly used for sporty gloves; frequently has an overcast or decorative stitch.

piqué
Wrong side lapped and sewn to right side so raw edge shows; allows for sleek finger look.

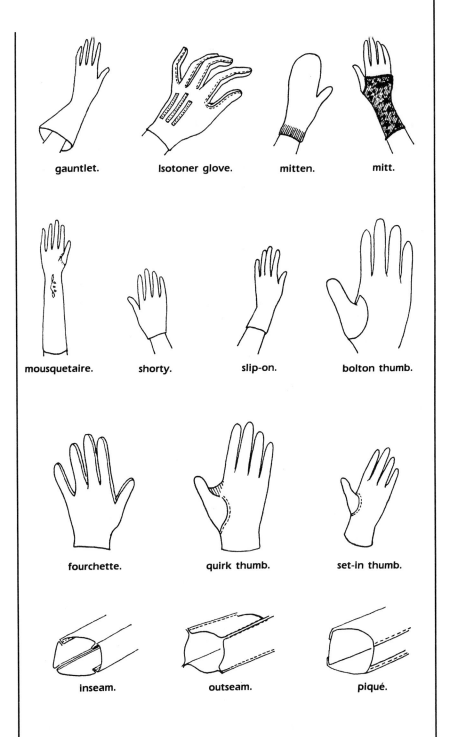

gauntlet.

Isotoner glove.

mitten.

mitt.

mousquetaire.

shorty.

slip-on.

bolton thumb.

fourchette.

quirk thumb.

set-in thumb.

inseam.

outseam.

piqué.

Hairstyles

A method of arranging hair. Other names include hairdo, headdress, and coiffure.

Afro
A dome-shaped hairdo created usually with kinky hair, combed straight out from head; adapted from natural hairstyle worn by Africans; popular in 1960s and 1970s for men and women.

artichoke
Layered, short haircut combed to back of head; popular in 1960s.

bangs
Hair combed over the forehead; can be straight or wavy.

Beatle cut
Men's full hairstyle popularized by the rock-music group the Beatles during the 1960s; characterized by long length in back, sideburns, and all-over fullness.

beehive
Exaggerated hairstyle; popular in the late 1950s through the mid-1960s; characterized by wide, high, dome-shaped back sweep.

bob
Short, smooth, blunt-cut hair worn close to the head.

bouffant
Very puffy women's hairstyle of the 1960s achieved by back-combing so that hair stands out from the head.

braid
The weaving together of three strands of hair in a crisscross fashion; most fashionable braided look of the 1980s was popularized by the actress Bo Derek in the movie *10*.

bun
A cluster of hair gathered to top or back of head and held in a ball form by pins or net cap.

Buster Brown
Short, straight cut with straight bangs over forehead; adapted as a popular hairstyle for boys from the early-twentieth-century comic-strip character Buster Brown.

crew cut
Close-cropped hairstyle worn generally by men; popular in the 1950s.

curls
Hair strands curved in various ways; types include:

barrel Full, round curls grouped at back of head.

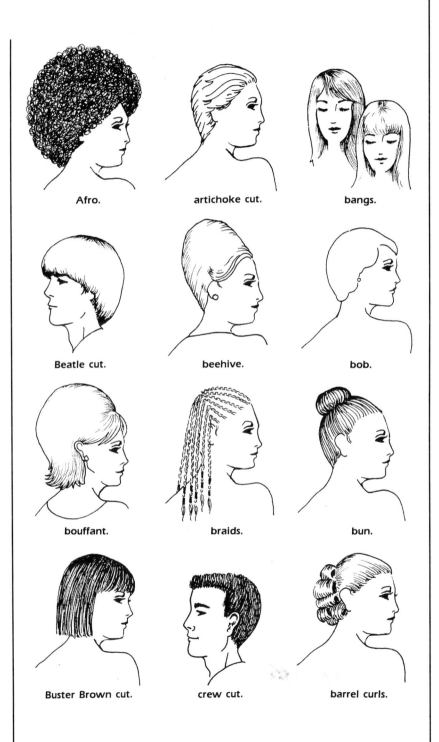

Afro.

artichoke cut.

bangs.

Beatle cut.

beehive.

bob.

bouffant.

braids.

bun.

Buster Brown cut.

crew cut.

barrel curls.

corkscrew Free-hanging tight spirals.

pin Small ringlets held close to the head with hair pins.

spit Flat ringlets used at forehead or cheek; often stiffened with hair lacquer to keep shape.

ducktail
Short hairstyle with a backward sweep that comes to a point at the neck; fashionable for both men and women in the 1950s and revived in 1970s and 1980s by Henry Winkler (Fonzie) on the television show *Happy Days*; also called a D.A.

fingerwave
Flat waves created with setting lotion and hair pins; popular in a short version in 1930s and early 1970s; also used on long hair in the late 1970s and early 1980s.

flip
Hairstyle of the 1960s, made popular by Jacqueline Kennedy, created by curling ends of hair outward.

French twist
Back of hair is swept up and held in place with a comb; popular in 1940s and a classic since then. Also called a French roll.

page boy
Smooth, straight, shoulder-length hairstyle curled under at back and sides; worn by boys in medieval times and popular for women in 1940s and 1970s.

pigtails
Two side braids; popular for girls.

pixie cut
Short, irregular-edged style; popular in late 1950s and early 1960s.

pompadour
Women's: A very high hairdo brushed away from the forehead over a stuffing roll. Named after Marquise de Pompadour, mistress of King Louis XV of France, popular in 1940s and 1960s.

Men's: Long hairstyle, brushed away from the forehead, without a part.

corkscrew curls.

pin curls.

spit curls.

ducktail.

fingerwaves.

flip.

French twist.

page boy.

pigtails.

pixie cut.

women's pompadour.

men's pompadour.

pony tail
Long hair pulled to top or back of head, then tied with an elastic band so that hair hangs down like a horse's tail; popular for young girls, especially in the 1950s.

poodle cut
Tight, kinky, short curls covering entire head; popular in 1950s, late 1970s and early 1980s.

shag
Long hair cut in layers and then curled outward; made popular in 1970s by actress Farrah Fawcett.

wedge
Above-the-shoulder hairstyle, made popular in the 1970s by ice-skating champion Dorothy Hamill; cut in a wedge shape at bottom.

Wigs

Synthetic materials such as modacrylic fiber or human hair used to create a full or partial head covering. Most popular styles include:

capless
Wig of any style that uses mesh straps as a foundation for the hair; provides better air circulation so wig is cooler to wear.

chignon
An extra hank of hair attached at top of head as a bun or twisted and attached at the back of head.

fall
Long hairpiece attached at hair crown.

mini fall
Short version of the fall.

switch
A long, straight hank of hair used to create a false ponytail, pigtails, braids, or other hairstyles.

toupee (too-*pay*)
A partial wig worn by men to cover baldness.

wiglet
A partial hank of hair added to create a fuller hairstyle or made into barrel curls and then attached to top or back of head; usually worn by women.

pony tail.

poodle cut.

shag.

wedge.

capless wig.

chignon.

fall.

switch.

toupee.

wiglet.

Hand Accessories

An item that complements apparel and is carried in the hand. The accessory can be decorative, functional, or both.

cane
A stick used as an aid in walking for both men and women. A fashionable accessory, particularly for men, from the sixteenth through the twentieth centuries. Materials used include rattan, malacca, bamboo, ebony, and ash; handle shapes and lengths vary.

swagger stick
Short stick, usually leather covered and shaped somewhat like a baton. Sometimes carried by army officers.

umbrella
Screen made of various materials and styles, designed for protection from sun and rain. Types include:

ballerina A ruffled edge trims a bell-shaped canopy.

bubble Long, dome-shaped canopy that covers head and shoulders; made of clear vinyl so wearer can see through it.

cocktail Small, decorative umbrella.

folding Ribs collapse in half, handle telescopes when in use. Its design makes it easy and convenient to carry.

golf Large, brightly colored canopy; usually has straight handle.

parasol Decorative umbrella to protect carrier from sun; style (a) popular in nineteenth and early twentieth centuries, usually has small canopy; style (b) used by Japanese, made of bamboo and brightly colored glazed paper.

Handbags

An accessory—also called purse, pocketbook, or bag—designed to carry personal belongings such as money and cosmetics. A variety of materials is used to construct the following styles:

accordion
Any style bag with pleated sides, an element of design frequently used on envelope-style bag (see below).

attaché case
Bag with rigid sides and top handle designed to carry papers, books, and other business needs. Used by men and women.

barrel
Soft, cyclinder-shaped bag; in 1980s, frequently made of "rip" fabric in very bright or metallic colors, also known as parachute bag.

canes.

parts of an umbrella.

spreaders

canopy

tips

ribs

shank

handle

swagger stick.

ballerina umbrella.

bubble umbrella.

cocktail umbrella.

folding umbrella.

golf umbrella.

parasols.

accordion bag.

attaché case.

barrel bag.

beaded
Any style bag covered with many types of beads; generally used as evening-wear accessory.

bookbag
Soft canvas bag used by schoolchildren to carry books; has either top or side handle. Also called schoolbag.

box
Rigid frame, square, or rectangular bag with rigid top handle.

briefcase
Soft rectangular bag with expandable sides; women's version has outside pockets, zippered top, and rigid top handle; men's version has envelope flap, latch closing, and rigid handle designed to carry business papers.

carpet
Satchel bag made of heavy tapestry fabric; adapted from the carpet valises used in travel after the Civil War; popular during the 1960s.

Chanel
Introduced in the late 1950s by designer Coco Chanel; made of soft quilted leather; adjustable shoulder chain strap.

change purse
Small bag used for carrying coins; some have rigid frame, others no frame and a zippered top.

clutch
Soft handbag with no handle.

duffel
A canvas bag with drawstring top; originally used by soldiers and sailors to carry personal belongings; adapted for use as beach bags and soft handbags.

envelope
Flat, rectangular bag shaped like business envelope.

French purse
Combination foldover wallet and change purse.

lunchbox
Box bag with dome-shaped top; frequently decorated with papier mâché or decoupage designs.

minaudiere (min-ode-ee-*air*)
Small, rigid evening bag covered with metallic fabric. Expensive versions made of genuine gold or silver metal.

muff
A warm bag designed to carry belongings and also keep hands warm; frequently made of fur.

parachute bag
See *barrel bag*.

pouch
Soft-sided bag with top handle.

schoolbag
See *bookbag*.

shoulder
Any style bag with long strap worn over the shoulder.

tote
Soft canvas open-top bag with top handles; used for shopping or carrying books and beach belongings.

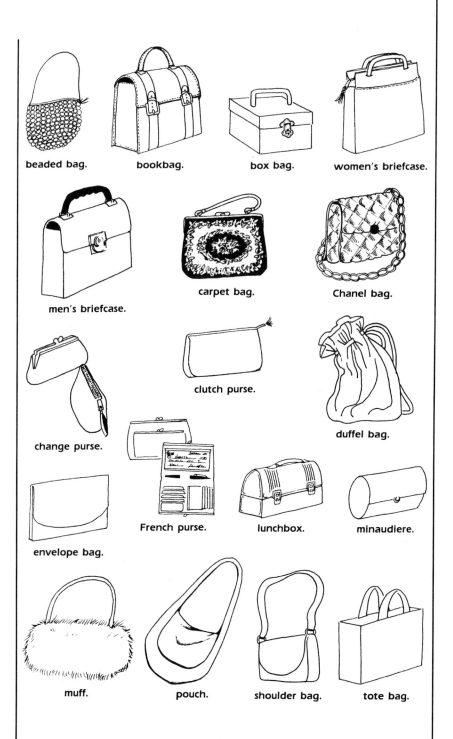

beaded bag.　　bookbag.　　box bag.　　women's briefcase.

men's briefcase.　　carpet bag.　　Chanel bag.

change purse.　　clutch purse.　　duffel bag.

envelope bag.　　French purse.　　lunchbox.　　minaudiere.

muff.　　pouch.　　shoulder bag.　　tote bag.

Hats

Covering for the head. Described by shapes and sizes of the crown and the brim. The crown is the part that sits directly on top of the head. The brim stands away from the head.

Alpine
See *Tyrolean.*

beret
Soft, round hat that folds flat off the head and is worn close to scalp, usually tilted to one side.

boater
Has flat brim, low crown, and ribbon band; made of straw and worn by men, women, and children; originally for boating.

bonnet
Soft hat made with or without a brim; usually made of a fabric such as percale; once worn by girls and women on the prairie as protective head covering; used frequently today as hat for babies.

bowler
Bowl-shaped crown with small brim rolled upwards at sides. Worn by men and women as part of riding attire; also called a derby.

Breton
Rounded crown hat with roll-up brim; worn by women and children.

calotte
Small cap that hugs the skull. Usually made of felt; also called a Juliet or a skullcap.

cartwheel
Women's hat with low crown and large flat brim; frequently used for wedding attire; also called a picture hat.

cloche
Deep-crowned hat that hugs the head closely; little or no brim; worn by the "flapper" girls of the 1920s, also fashionable during the 1960s.

coolie
Wide, cone-shaped hat worn by the Chinese rice-field workers, called "coolies"; usually made of bamboo; fashionable in the late 1970s and early 1980s.

cossack
Tall, brimless hat worn by Russian men; usually made of fur; fashionable in the 1970s.

cowboy
Has high crown with center crease and medium or wide brim; worn by American cowboys; fashionable in late 1970s and 1980s for young men and women.

derby
See *bowler.*

fedora
Creased-crown and curved-brim hat usually made of felt; also called a homburg; worn by both men and women.

fez
Cone-shaped brimless hat with flat top; long silk tassel usually attached at top.

gaucho
Low-circular-crown, wide-brim hat adapted from the South American cowboy; fashionable in the 1970s and worn with gaucho pants by women.

halo
Circular, brimmed hat with low crown; worn off the forehead, it forms a circle around the head.

parts of the hat: 1. the crown; 2. the brim.

beret.

boater.

bonnet.

bowler.

Breton cap.

calotte.

cartwheel hat.

cloche.

coolie hat.

cossack hat.

cowboy hat.

fedora.

fez.

gaucho hat.

halo hat.

helmet
Brimless hat that encircles the entire head and snaps together under chin; usually constructed of a rigid material.

homburg
See *fedora*.

hood
Soft head covering worn by men, women, and children, particularly with active sportswear or for general warmth. Frequently attached to above-the-waist garment, either permanently or with zipper.

jockey cap
Small, close-fitting crown with small, visor-type brim; generally worn with sports attire by men, women, and children.

Juliet
See *calotte*.

mushroom
Large brim turned downwards on the face; very fashionable in 1960s for women.

panama
Creased low-crown hat with brim turned upwards in back; made of a straw from the leaves of a jipijapa plant.

picture
See *cartwheel*.

pillbox
Small, round, brimless hat that sits on top of head; fashionable for women in the 1930s, 1950s, and 1960s.

pith
See *topee*.

profile
Low-crown and circular-brim hat worn to the side of the face; fashionable for women in the 1940s.

safari
See *topee*.

sailor
Small, round, gored-crown hat with upturned brim; American sailor hat made of white duck; can also be styled like the boater and made of straw.

skullcap
See *calotte*.

slouch
Soft hat with a flexible brim; usually worn by women.

tam or tam o'shanter
Soft, round hat that is gathered into a head band; worn to one side or on back of the head; usually has a pom-pom on top.

top
Stiff crown, small, stiff brim with small roll at sides; generally made of silk; worn by men with formal attire.

topee *or* topi
Stiff, sectioned-crown hat with stiff downturn brim; worn in tropical climates as protection from the sun; fashionable in the 1980s; also called a safari hat, pith hat, or pith helmet.

toque
Small, round, brimless hat worn close to head by women.

turban
Soft, draped hat that covers the entire head.

Tyrolean
Soft felt hat with cone-shaped crown, small brim that turns up on one side; usually worn by men; sometimes called Alpine hat.

helmet.

hood.

jockey cap.

mushroom hat.

panama.

pillbox hat.

profile hat.

sailor hat.

slouch hat.

tam *or* tam o'shanter.

topee *or* topi.

top hat.

toque.

turban.

Tyrolean hat.

Hosiery

Accessories that cover all or part of the legs.

anklets
Short socks that end just above the ankle; worn by men, women, and children.

argyle socks
Diagonal-plaid socks worn by men, women, and children; fashionable for students in the 1930s.

bobby socks
Anklets made of thick knitted fabric with tops folded over; fashionable in the 1950s. A classic for schoolgirls; frequently worn by school cheerleaders.

body stocking
Knitted one-piece garment that covers body from neck to feet; slit or snaps at crotch; fashionable in the 1960s for women; worn under see-through dresses and mini skirts.

body suit
See *leotard.*

fishnet hose
Panty hose made of open-work mesh fabric; frequently worn by dancers; fashionable in the 1960s and 1970s.

footlets
Sheer nylon or coarse-knit fabric that covers foot only; elasticized at edge for snug fit. Sheer type worn in place of panty hose. Heavy fabric type used as a slipper.

full-fashioned
Tucks or fashion marks created in hosiery that is knitted flat with increase or decrease in stitches and then seamed together.

knee socks
Medium- to heavy-gauge knits that cover legs from foot to just below knee; worn by men, women, and children. Sheer knits are called knee highs.

leg warmers
Long tubes of bulky knit that cover leg from ankle to upper thigh; worn by dancers; fashionable over pants and under skirts for teenagers in the 1980s.

leotard
One-piece knitted, tight-fitting cover-up of torso; can be sleeveless, short sleeved, or long sleeved; variation called body suit or body shirt.

panty hose
Stockings with attached panty, generally of same knit; worn by women and girls; support-top pantyhose have power elastic in the panty section; opaque knit hose called tights; said to be textured when made of lacy or decorative knit.

slipper socks
Vinyl or fabric foot covering with knitted sock attached. Worn by men, women, and children for warmth and comfort.

support hose
Elasticized stocking of any style, designed to hold leg muscles tight; worn by men and women.

sweat socks
Heavy-gauge knit used by men, women, and children for athletics; some contain extra padding in the foot to absorb perspiration.

textured hose
See *panty hose.*

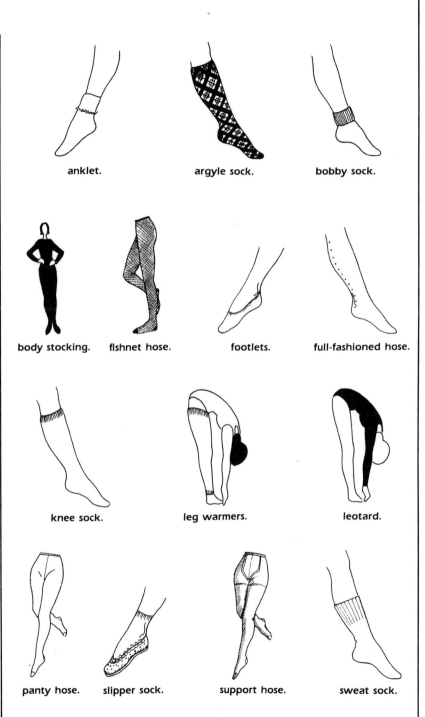

anklet.

argyle sock.

bobby sock.

body stocking.

fishnet hose.

footlets.

full-fashioned hose.

knee sock.

leg warmers.

leotard.

panty hose.

slipper sock.

support hose.

sweat sock.

thigh highs

Sheer hose that ends in elastic band at midthigh; worn by women.

tights

see *panty hose.*

tube socks

Socks knitted with rib stitches in one long tube without shaped foot; worn by men, women, and children, particularly for athletics.

Jewelry

An ornament that decorates the body. Sometimes used as a symbol of social status, for example, a wedding ring.

bracelets

Arm or foot bands of various types. Types include:

ankle Fine chain worn around the ankle; frequently has ornament or stone attached.

bangle Circular band worn at wrist or forearm; made of a wide variety of materials (gold, silver, wood, plastic, papier mâché, and so forth).

charm Chain bracelet with dangling ornaments attached.

identification (ID) Chain linked to a flat band that has a name or message engraved; usually made of gold, silver, or copper.

snake Mesh coil that winds around the arm; usually worn on upper arm with a snake head as an ornament.

watch Circular band that conceals watch housing.

earrings

Ornaments used to decorate the ear; usually worn by women. Types include:

ball Dome-shaped bead, stone, or metal set on a pierced, screw, or clip base.

button Circular earring, attached to any type base; button made of pearls or plastic.

chandelier Decorative dangling earring.

thigh highs.

tube socks.

ankle bracelet.

bangle bracelet.

charm bracelet.

identification bracelet.

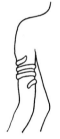

snake bracelet.

watch.

ball earrings.

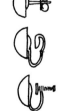

button earrings.

chandelier earrings.

clip Top can be any shape; back has spring clip to hold earring on the ear.

drop Lower part of earring drops from the base.

hoop Wire circle usually made of gold or silver metal.

pierced Any shape ornament attached to a gold wire that goes straight through a hole in the ear; cap or catch at end holds earring in place.

screw Any shape ornament attached to a two-piece base that screws onto the back of the ear.

necklaces
A wide variety of materials worn around the neck; used by men, women, and children. Types include:

bib Multiple strands graduated to form a bib shape; frequently made of pearls or imitation stones.

choker Tight band worn high on the neck; frequently made of circular beads.

dog collar Worn the same as choker but made of ribbon with ornament attached.

lavaliere A pendant or ornament attached to a chain, ribbon, or cord.

locket Small case suspended on a chain or cord; opens to reveal a photograph of a loved one.

matinee length Pearl or bead necklace 30 to 35 inches long.

opera length Pearl or bead necklace 48 to 120 inches long.

rope Matinee or opera length wrapped around neck or knotted midway.

pins
Wire with attached ornament used to fasten and/or decorate apparel. Types include:

brooch (broach) Pin with ornament attached; used for decorative purposes on women's apparel.

cuff link Wire stem with ornament attached; stem bends in half to hold French cuffs together; usually on men's shirts.

hat Long, sharp-pointed, with ornament at the end; used to secure a woman's hat to her head. Also serves as a decoration.

safety Spring-activated clasp covers pointed edge wire; used to fasten items together but can be decorative as well; holds together cloth diapers and kilts.

scatter Small pin worn in a cluster with other similar pins.

stick Long wire with ornament at one end and cap at the other; frequently worn in women's jacket lapels.

tie bar Ornament used to hold tie ends together; has clip on reverse side that can be clipped to man's shirt.

tie tack Short wire with ornament at one end and cap at the other; frequently has chain tying two parts together; used to hold two ends of men's ties together; ornament end shows on front of tie.

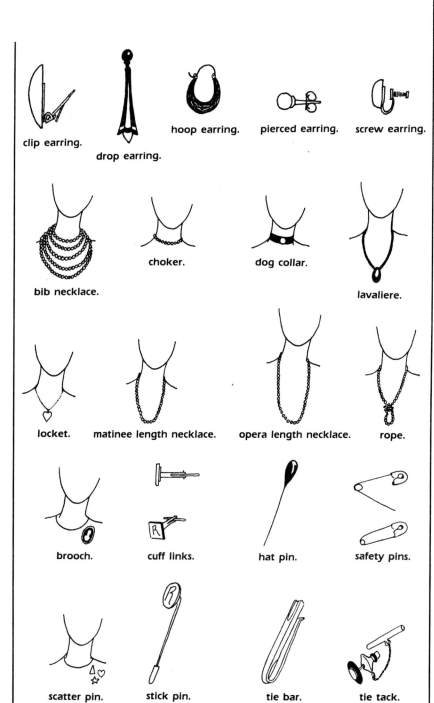

clip earring.

drop earring.

hoop earring.

pierced earring.

screw earring.

bib necklace.

choker.

dog collar.

lavaliere.

locket.

matinee length necklace.

opera length necklace.

rope.

brooch.

cuff links.

hat pin.

safety pins.

scatter pin.

stick pin.

tie bar.

tie tack.

ring
Decorative ornament that circles one or more fingers of the hand. The outside design on a ring is called a ring style. Ring styles include:

class Usually contains a colored stone set into an engraved school design; may be a signet; worn by students attending high schools and colleges.

dinner Contains a combination of large and small stones; long in shape and worn on the little finger; also called a cocktail ring.

engagement Usually a solitaire diamond worn by women on the third finger, left hand, as a symbol of their intended marriage.

wedding Circular band made usually of gold; with or without stones or engraving; worn by married men and women on third finger of left hand.

ring setting styles
Stones may be attached, or set, onto rings in the following styles:

channel Stones set in a long, narrow channel; commonly used for wedding rings.

fishtail A low, long row of prongs holding a series of stones, as in a wedding or dinner ring.

flush Metal edge is smooth against a circle stone; frequently seen in class rings.

Tiffany Six prongs hold a solitaire stone.

hair ornaments
A decoration worn in the hair by women and children; also used to hold hair in place. Types include:

barrette Decorative clip for the hair; made of plastic, metals, straw, or other materials; designed to hold hair off the face.

bobby pin U-shape wire with one flat side and one ridged side; used to hold hair up as in a bun or swept off the face; can also have decorative tip.

hair band Ribbon or fabric that circles the head from crown to neck.

hair sticks Long, pointed sticks of wood, metal, or plastic that slide into a barrette-type clip; used to hold hair twisted in back of head, adapted from the costume of the Japanese geisha girl.

tiara Circular crown worn on top of head for formal occasions or weddings; usually made of rhinestones or pearls.

class ring.

dinner ring.

engagement ring.

wedding ring.

channel setting.

fishtail setting.

flush setting.

Tiffany setting.

barrette.

bobby pin.

hair band.

hair sticks.

tiara.

Neckwear

Articles of dress worn around the neck to complement other apparel.

ascot
Wide tie looped loosely around the neck and held in place with tie tack or stick pin. Traditionally worn by men, particularly with formal attire; today also worn by women.

bandanna
Traditionally, red or blue large cotton square folded into a triangle and tied around the neck. Has distinctive white or black print. Worn with railroad-worker uniform or the American cowboy attire.

boa
Long, narrow scarf made of fur or feathers and draped around a woman's neck for a glamorous touch.

bolo tie
Thin tie made of cording; capped at ends with metal tips and held together with decorative slide; frequently worn with Western shirts, particularly by men.

bow tie
Straight, narrow band tied in a bow

under man's chin; frequently used for formal wear.

cravat
Rectangular scarf tied at neck; ends are tucked inside shirt; worn by men in place of a necktie.

dickey
Partial collar or neckline worn by men, women, and children under a shirt, blouse, or dress to accent the other garment or give additional warmth.

four-in-hand
The most common tie worn by men today; tied in a flat knot at neck; long strands hang down.

kerchief
Square scarf folded in a triangle and tied at head or neck. Commonly worn by women.

smoke ring
Rectangular scarf cut on the bias and sewn at ends to form a continuous tube; worn by women; fashionable in the 1960s.

Windsor tie
Similar to the men's four-in-hand tie but having oversized knot.

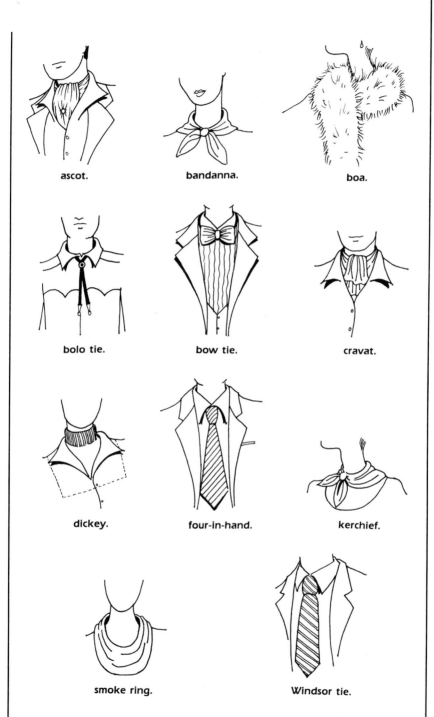

ascot.

bandanna.

boa.

bolo tie.

bow tie.

cravat.

dickey.

four-in-hand.

kerchief.

smoke ring.

Windsor tie.

Accessory Fabrics and Materials

The materials defined in this section are used for belts, boots, shoes, slippers, gloves, hand accessories, handbags, hats, jewelry, neckwear, and sometimes apparel.

alligator
Leather characterized by irregular boxlike markings with a glossy surface. Most alligator designs used today are cowhide stamped to look like an alligator skin. Generally used for shoes, handbags, and wallets.

beads
Variety of shaped pieces of glass, plastic, wood, precious and semiprecious stones, and other materials that have been sewn to a background fabric. Used on a variety of accessories.

braided straw
Natural or synthetic straw intertwined in strips and then joined together. Usually used for handbags and hats.

canvas
A popular casual, heavy, durable fabric usually made of cotton fiber used for shoes, handbags, and hats.

chamois
Skin from a sheep that is oil dressed and resembles suede. Used for accessories and apparel.

deerskin
Porous, stretchy, fine-textured leather used for handbags, gloves, and trims.

felt
Nonwoven fabric made by compressing wool and other fibers. Generally used for hats.

glazed kidskin
Young goatskins that are coated. Very soft leather. Used for garments, shoes, gloves, handbags, and belts.

Gore-Tex
Trademark name of a coating put on a woven fabric to make it waterproof yet breathable; usually used on boots.

lizard
Skin with narrow, irregularly shaped rectangular design. Frequently used for shoes, handbags, and belts.

mesh
A flexible material made of linked metal, flat beads of gold or silver, or plated metal. Most often used for handbags.

Morocco
A vegetable-tanned goatskin with a fine pebbly texture. Used for all types of accessories.

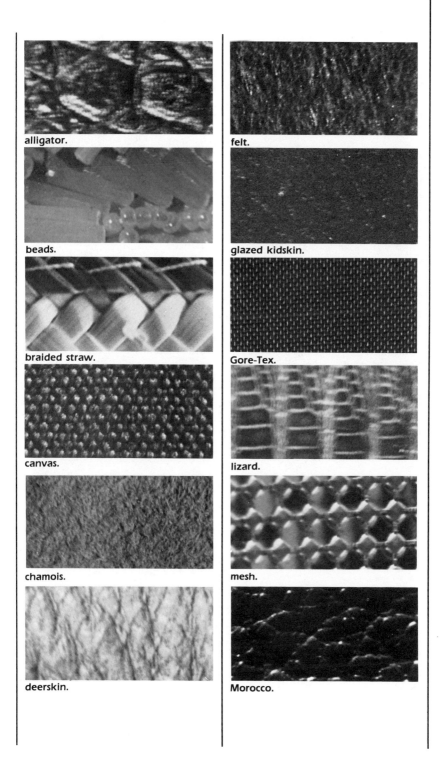

alligator.

felt.

beads.

glazed kidskin.

braided straw.

Gore-Tex.

canvas.

lizard.

chamois.

mesh.

deerskin.

Morocco.

ostrich
Highly valued because it is quite rare. The unique texture is characterized by quill-like dotted projections, which produce a two-tone appearance after tanning. Used for small items like wallets and key cases.

patent leather
Usually a cowhide leather with a glossy finish created by coating with a glaze; sometimes the glaze is a plastic coating.

pigskin
A very durable leather from a pig; characterized by tiny pin-size holes on the surface. Used for handbags, shoes, and belts.

rip stop
A very closely woven fabric with coarse filling and warp yarns placed at regular intervals. Usually made of nylon fiber and used for handbags.

snakeskin
Skins from cobras, pythons, rattlesnakes, boas and others, characterized by a diamond-shape scale on the surface of the skin. Used for all types of accessories and some apparel.

squash patent
Crinkled surface added to patent leather for interest. Used in many types of accessories.

suede
Flesh side of an animal skin that has light nap surface; cowhide or kidskin frequently used for many types of accessories.

synthetic straw
A plastic made to look like natural straw; used for hats and handbags.

tapestry
A woven fabric with a pictorial design interlaced in the fabric. Frequently used for handbags.

vinyl
Plastic sheet of a smooth or rough texture, which resembles leather. Used for many types of accessories.

wicker straw
Stiff, rod-shaped straw that is usually interlaced for handbags.

willow straw
Soft, ropelike straw used in crocheted handbags, hats, and shoes.

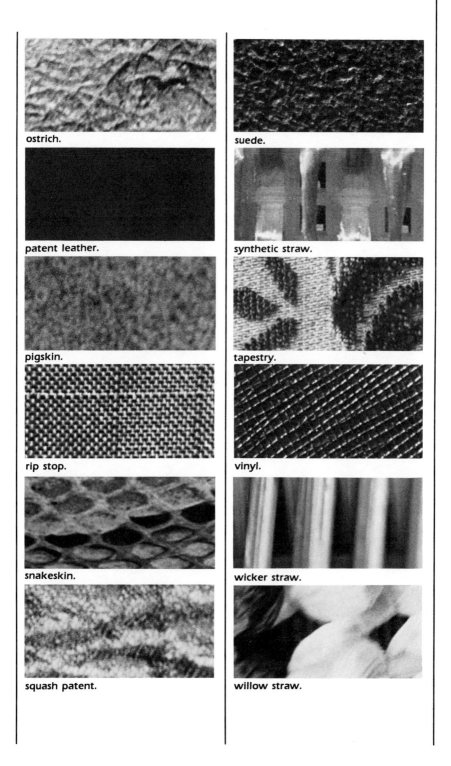

ostrich.

suede.

patent leather.

synthetic straw.

pigskin.

tapestry.

rip stop.

vinyl.

snakeskin.

wicker straw.

squash patent.

willow straw.

5

Clothing Components

Buttons
Trims
Collars
Necklines
Pockets
Sleeves

Buttons

An object used to fasten or decorate a garment, a button is formed into a circle, square, triangle, or oblong or other shape. Common materials used for buttons include bone, metal, glass, plastic, fabric, shells, jewels, wood, and leather. Types include:

ball
Circular button; varieties include full ball, half ball, and quarter ball.

Chinese
Button made of a series of corded loops; cording can be of a self fabric (same fabric as garment), covered cord, or soutache braid; frequently used on Chinese-style shirts and jackets.

covered
Generally a shank button covered with garment self fabric or contrasting fabric.

crocheted
Crochet loops arranged to form a ball button; sometimes contains molded center to maintain shape.

flat
Button top is thin; types include shankless two- or four-hole and shank.

overall
Two-part button usually made of metal and used to attach shoulder strap to bib of overalls.

shank
Any type button with projection of metal or plastic used to secure button on garment.

tubular toggle
Oblong button frequently used with frog or toggle closings.

Trims

Decorative items attached to a garment or an accessory. Types include:

appliqué (ap-li-*kay*)
A design applied to another surface, frequently with a decorative stitch. Sometimes contains quilt padding for a dimensional effect.

braid
Cord or flat strip used to trim a garment. Very heavy embroidered types called passementerie (pas-mehn-*tree*). Types include:

middy Very narrow braid used to trim middy blouses or tailored coats and suits.

military Flat braid made of diagonal twill weave, frequently of gold color; used to decorate military uniforms.

plait Crisscross cording, as in a hair braid; used as an edging or sometimes as a belt.

rickrack *or* ricrac Zigzag braid trim; used as an edging on aprons and children's and women's garments.

soutache (soo-*tach*) Narrow, round decorative braid; frequently used at edge of a sailor collar.

buttonhole
Opening through which a button is passed to secure garment or accessory parts. Types include:

bound Hole edged with fabric, braid, or leather; usually seen on women's tailored garments.

eyelet Circular buttonhole edged with close zigzag stitch; frequently used with tie-type garment closings

full ball

Chinese button.

covered button.

half ball

quarter ball

ball buttons.

crocheted button.

flat button.

overall button.

shank buttons.

tubular toggles.

appliqué.

middy.

military braid.

plait.

rickrack *or* ricrac.

soutache.

bound buttonhole.

eyelet buttonhole.

or fabric belts, for women's, children's, or men's apparel.

frog-toggle Decorative cording attached to front of garment; one side forms loop buttonhole and the other holds the button; derived from native Chinese costumes.

loop Constructed from a cord, fabric, or crochet thread and attached at edge of garment to hold buttons; traditionally used as a back closing on wedding gowns.

piped A bound buttonhole with corded edge; frequently edged with a contrasting color.

slot An opening in a seam, used as a buttonhole.

tailored Opening stitched with close machine zigzag stitch; also called worked buttonhole.

edging
A trim applied to edge or border of an apparel or accessory item. Types include:

bias Self or contrasting fabric cut on diagonal grain and attached to edge.

crochet Lace edge achieved with crochet thread; frequently used on lingerie and apparel for young girls.

embroidery Decorative stitching superimposed on fabric with contrasting thread; any design can be used.

lettuce Rippled edge formed by stretching fabric as it is sewn with a machine zigzag stitch; also called marrow edge.

picot (*pee*-co) A series of tiny loops decorating an edge; frequently used on ribbons and lingerie.

piping Narrow cord or bias fabric stitched between a seam; made of matching or contrasting fabric color.

scallops A series of circular curves frequently used as hem edge.

sequins
Plastic disks sewn to garment to give decorative sparkle; usually used for women's evening garments.

studs
Decorative metal ornaments hammered onto a garment; frequently used on Western-style and theatrical garments.

tucks
Parallel folds of fabric stitched on outside or inside of garment; called pin tucks when many tucks are used close together with a narrow fold.

quilting
Three layers (top, padding, and lining) of fabric used to give a puffy appearance; layers are held together with a variety of quilt-design stitching; whole or part of garment can be quilted.

ribbon
A narrow, flat, or tubular piece of closely woven fabric used as a trim. Types include:

embroidered Ribbon decorated with a thread design; used to trim women's and children's apparel; sometimes worn as a hair ornament.

grosgrain (*gro*-grain) Heavy ribbon with crosswise ribs.

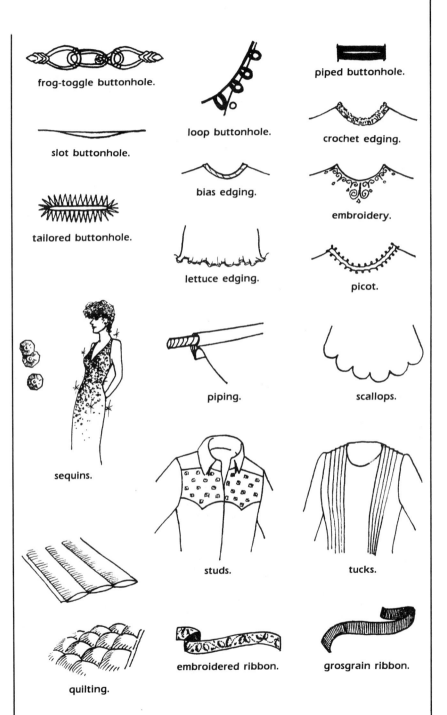

frog-toggle buttonhole.

loop buttonhole.

piped buttonhole.

slot buttonhole.

crochet edging.

bias edging.

embroidery.

tailored buttonhole.

lettuce edging.

picot.

sequins.

piping.

scallops.

studs.

tucks.

quilting.

embroidered ribbon.

grosgrain ribbon.

satin Ribbon made of satin-weave fabric distinguished by a shiny surface, as in bottom-weight fabrics.

velvet Pile-weave fabric as in bottom-weight fabrics, made into ribbon form.

ruffles
Strip of fabric that forms a ripple at edge of garment. Types include:

bias Edging made from circular pieces of fabric; smooth at seam edge, fuller at hem edge.

gathered Edging made from strip of straight-grain fabric; fullness, same at seam and hem edge, is created by gathering or pleating fabric.

seams
Two edges of fabric joined or edged in the following ways:

bound Bias tape encased over the raw edges on inside of garment; frequently used on unlined jacket seams.

corded A plain seam with bias-covered cord inserted in middle; sometimes used on the outseam of jeans.

fagoting The joining of two pieces of fabric with embroidery thread to create a lacy design. Also a type of embroidery stitch.

flat-felled Two fabrics joined wrong sides together: one edge is trimmed close to stitching, the other is turned under and top stitched. From the right side, two rows of stitching are visible. Commonly used on shirts, blouses, and jeans.

French Wrong sides are joined together, then turned and stitched again on inside; raw edge completely en-closed inside seam; frequently used on transparent fabrics.

lap Edges of fabric placed one over the other without edges being turned under; frequently used on leather, suede, and ultrasuede garments and accessories.

overcast Raw edges finished with a zigzag stitch; also called serged seam.

pinked Raw edges of seam cut with saw-tooth shears to prevent fabric from unraveling.

piped See *piping* under *edging*.

plain Fabrics are joined right sides together; the most common seam used in garment construction.

serged See *overcast*.

strap Plain seam sewn with wrong sides together and raw edges covered with bias tape; used for reinforcement and decorative purposes.

top stitched A plain seam pressed open, with one or more rows of stitching on either side of the seam line.

welt Plain seam with two raw edges pressed to one side and top stitched close to seam line.

smocking
An embroidered thread sewn on top-gathered folds of fabric; frequently used on infants' and girls' apparel.

trapunto
Multiple rows of stitches that create a padded, quilted effect; used on belts, neckline trims, and hemlines of women's apparel.

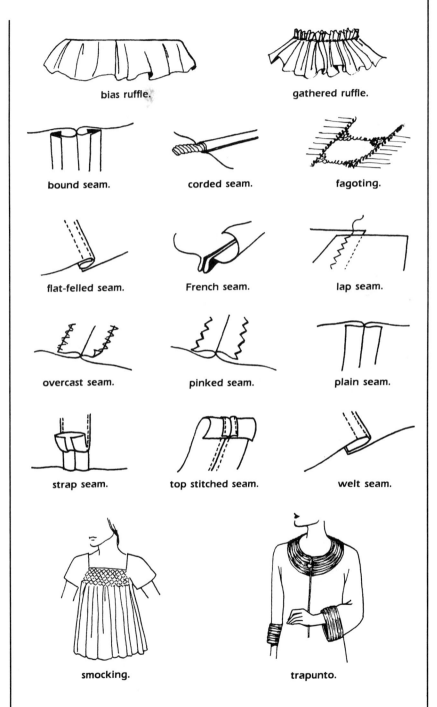

bias ruffle.

gathered ruffle.

bound seam.

corded seam.

fagoting.

flat-felled seam.

French seam.

lap seam.

overcast seam.

pinked seam.

plain seam.

strap seam.

top stitched seam.

welt seam.

smocking.

trapunto.

Collars

Separate piece of fabric or other material that finishes or decorates the neckline of clothing. Illustrated are parts of collar used in definitions.

band
Narrow strip cut on straight grain or bias grain of fabric; used frequently on men's shirts and ladies' blouses.

Barrymore
Sits low in front with points 4½ to 5 inches long; named for actor John Barrymore; popular during 1920s and 1930s.

belmont
High-band, short, starched collar, with rounded ends; used from 1910 to 1920 on men's shirts.

Bermuda
Narrow, rounded collar with straight front edge; sometimes called a Dutch collar; a classic style for women's and children's blouses and dresses.

bertha
Deep, flat collar that falls from neckline to shoulder opening at front or back.

bib
Round, square, or oval shape fitting around neck like child's bib; usually a separate piece worn over a dress.

bow
Straight strip tied in a bow; popular collar for women's blouses and dresses; fashionable in the late 1970s and early 1980s.

Buster Brown
Stiff, medium-sized collar with a rounded front fall popularized by comic strip character in early 1900s; used for children's apparel (particularly uniforms) and women's apparel.

button-down
Pointed collar with ends that button to body of shirt, blouse, or dress; commonly used on men's shirts in 1950s and 1980s.

cadet
See *Chinese*.

cape
Large circular-cut collar that usually extends from shoulders.

Chelsea
Flat collar formed from a V neckline; long, pointed ends at front; popular during 1960s and revived in 1980s.

Chinese
A band collar that stands straight at neck edge, about 1 inch high, and opens at center front; also called mandarin, cadet, or Nehru collar.

choker
See *dog*.

Continental
Rounded-edge, narrow-rolled collar, cut away sharply at sides; used on men's shirts in 1950s, 1960s, and 1980s.

convertible
Any tailored collar that can be worn open or closed; frequently called man-tailored.

cossack
High-standing collar similar to Chinese or band but closing at side, frequently trimmed with embroidery; also known as Zhivago collar and Russian collar.

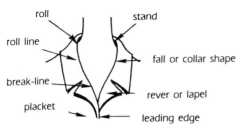

parts of a collar.

roll
stand
roll line
break-line
placket
fall or collar shape
rever or lapel
leading edge

band collar.

Barrymore collar.

belmont collar.

Bermuda collar.

bertha collar.

bib collar.

bow collar.

Buster Brown collar.

button-down collar.

cape collar.

Chelsea collar.

Chinese collar.

Continental collar.

convertible collars.

cossack collar.

cowl
Large, circular, draped collar frequently cut on the bias; usually used on women's apparel.

dog
Tight-fitted band high about the neck base; sometimes called a choker collar.

Dutch
See *Bermuda.*

eyelet
High-roll or tab-type collar with rounded or angle edges containing eyelets for pin insert; popular on men's shirts in 1930s and 1960s.

hood
Soft draped collar that also serves as a soft head covering; when used on coats, frequently lined with natural or synthetic fur.

jabot (jha-*bow*)
Hanging ruffle attached to front of collar, either permanent or detachable; used on men's formal wear, ladies' blouses and dresses, and children's wear.

Johnny
Small, flat collar frequently used on shirts and shirtwaist dresses.

mandarin
See *Chinese.*

man-tailored
See *convertible* or *tailored shirt.*

middy
See *sailor.*

mock turtle
Separate band stitched down to simulate a turtleneck collar; often knitted.

Nehru
Similar to Chinese collar but sometimes made with rounded corners; named after costume worn by prime minister of India Jawaharlal Nehru; popular during 1960s.

Peter Pan
Flat round collar usually 2 to 3 inches wide, having round ends; popular in children's wear.

Pierrot
A ruffled collar derived from French pantomime comedian Pierrot's costume; authentic costume collar contains two rows of ruffles; adaptations contain one row of ruffles.

Pilgrim
See *Puritan.*

portrait
A low-standing collar attached to a scooped neckline.

Puritan
Flat, wide collar with pointed ends; similar to collar worn by Puritans; also called Pilgrim collar.

ring
Stand-up collar that circles neck; also called wedding-band collar.

rolled
High collar at back; rolls gently away from neck at front.

Roman
Straight, high band that snaps or buttons in back.

Russian
See *cossack.*

sailor
Patterned after collar worn by American sailors; square at back, forming

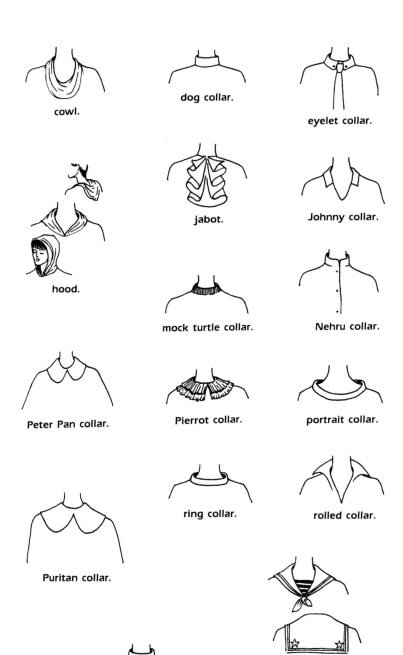

cowl.

dog collar.

eyelet collar.

hood.

jabot.

Johnny collar.

mock turtle collar.

Nehru collar.

Peter Pan collar.

Pierrot collar.

portrait collar.

ring collar.

rolled collar.

Puritan collar.

sailor collar.

Roman collar.

a V at front; usually trimmed with braid and having detachable dickey and tie.

shawl
A soft roll collar cut with body of garment and seamed at back; sometimes lapel section is notched.

spread
A man's basic shirt collar made with wide division between points in front; made to accommodate Windsor knot tie; also called Windsor collar.

tab
Shirt collar with two flaps attached to ends to hold points of collar close to shirt; tab also called mechanical stand.

tailored shirt
A basic collar cut in two sections: a band section and an upper collar. The upper collar can be square, round, or rectangular.

turtleneck
A high band collar that folds over once or twice; often made of knitted fabric.

tuxedo
Similar to shawl collar but extends to entire length of garment.

wedding-band
See *ring.*

Windsor
See *spread.*

winged
A high-standing, usually stiff collar with long, pointed tips.

Zhivago
See *cossack.*

Necklines

The term *neckline* refers to an outline of the neck area. Types include:

bateau (bah-*tow*)
Also called a boat; cut in shallow curve from shoulder to shoulder.

built-up
Neckline extends above base of neck 1 inch or more.

camisole
Neckline formed straight above bustline, bodice held up by straps over shoulder.

cardigan
High, plain, round neckline that opens by buttons along center front.

crew
Round, high, close-fitted neckline used on knitted sweaters; usually rib knit.

decolletage *or* decolleté (day-kol-eh-*tay*)
Low-cut neckline that starts off the shoulder and falls low in front to bustline.

drawstring
Cord used to gather fullness either high or low on the neck; other names include peasant or gypsy.

Florentine
Extends from shoulder straight across front and back; inspired by Renaissance painters.

gypsy
See *drawstring.*

halter
Strap, band, or rope that holds backless garment at neck.

shawl collar.

spread collar.

tab collar.

tailored shirt collar.

turtleneck.

tuxedo collar.

winged collar.

bateau neck.

built-up neck.

camisole neck.

cardigan neck.

crew neck.

decolletage *or* decolleté.

drawstring neck.

Florentine neck.

halter neck.

horseshoe
Low, scooped in front like a horse-shoe.

jewel
Simple, round, plain neckline suitable for many types of neck jewelry.

keyhole
Keyholelike opening at front of garment; can be rounded or wedge shape.

one-shoulder
Asymmetric line that extends diagonally over one shoulder to underarm of opposite side. Classic, and still popular in the 1970s and 1980s.

peasant
See *drawstring*.

plunging
In women's apparel, low cut, usually to waist, revealing part of breasts.

scoop
Low, rounded, curved neckline.

square
Angular, perpendicular cut, as in a square.

strapless
Having no shoulders or straps.

sweetheart
Deep cut such that a heart shape results.

V-shaped
Cut like the letter V.

Pockets

Separate section of material sewn to a garment or accessory to form a pouch; can be sewn on inside or outside. Types include:

bellows
Patch-type pocket with inverted or box pleat to allow for expansion; used on jackets, shirts, and safari-style garments; also called safari pocket.

bound
Outside of pocket opens like a bound buttonhole to reveal a concealed inner pocket; also called a piped, slash, slit, or slot pocket.

envelope
Pocket is attached to outside of garment or accessory with flap and pleated sides; frequently used on handbags, luggage, and aprons.

flap
Any type pocket with separate covering at the top.

fob
See *watch* pocket.

key
Small patch pocket sewn inside a larger pocket to hold keys or coins; frequently seen on jeans and men's pants.

mock
A flap sewn on outside garment that looks like a pocket but is not.

patch
Pocket attached on outside of garment.

piped
See *bound*.

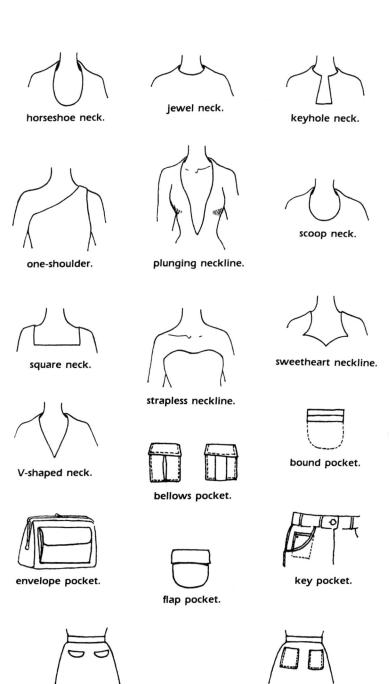

horseshoe neck.

jewel neck.

keyhole neck.

one-shoulder.

plunging neckline.

scoop neck.

square neck.

strapless neckline.

sweetheart neckline.

V-shaped neck.

bellows pocket.

bound pocket.

envelope pocket.

flap pocket.

key pocket.

mock pocket.

patch pocket.

safari
See *bellows*.

seam
Inside pocket attached to both sides of seam; can be top stitched on outside or left free.

slash
See *bound*.

slit
See *bound*.

slot
See *bound*.

vest
A small welt pocket used near waist-line or chest of men's or women's vests; originally used to hold a pocket watch.

watch pocket
A small inside slot or welt pocket attached to men's or women's pants at waistline; originally used to hold a pocket watch; today used on jeans and other pants as a decorative detail and to hold keys, coins, and other small items.

welt
Type of bound pocket with one edge of binding wider than the other. Used on Continental pants and tailored suits and skirts for men's and women's apparel.

Sleeves

That part of a garment that covers the arm; can be a separate attached piece or an extension of the garment. Types include:

batwing
Long sleeve with wide armhole and narrow wrist; can be cut in one piece with garment or as a separate section.

bell
Smooth fitting at armhole; flares to hem edge like a bell.

bishop
Long sleeve with fullness held by cuff at wrist; armhole edge can be flat or gathered.

circular cap
Short sleeve that flares out from armhole edge in a circle.

dolman
Similar to batwing sleeve but fuller at underarm.

drop shoulder
Shoulder seam extends 2 to 4 inches over the upper arm; any type of sleeve can be attached.

epaulet (ep-a-*let*)
A tab cut as part of shoulder and sleeve or a separate section; can also be used at hem edge for roll-up sleeves.

fitted
A narrow sleeve made from one or two pieces and set into a small arm-hole. The effect gives a tight fit from shoulder to wrist that is desirable in tailored garments.

seam pocket.

vest pocket.

watch pocket.

welt pocket.

batwing sleeve.

bell sleeve.

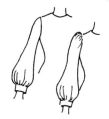

bishop sleeve.

circular cap sleeve.

dolman sleeve.

drop shoulder sleeve.

epaulet.

fitted sleeves.

Juliet *or* **Juliette**
Long sleeve with puffy top and fitted bottom; named after William Shakespeare's heroine Juliet.

kimono
Long or short sleeve cut in one with body of garment; derived from Japanese kimono; sometimes a separate section called a gusset is added at underarm.

lantern
A two-piece sleeve that is narrow at armhole and hem and wide through the arm.

leg-o'-mutton
Sleeve with puff at the armhole edge achieved through gathers or tucks and narrow at hem edge; fashionable in 1940s and 1980s; generally used on women's garments.

melon
Short, full sleeve made in sections to create a puff at arm center; sometimes made of transparent fabric or stiffened for an exaggerated effect; frequently used on women's garments.

peasant
Full gathered sleeve with elastic hem edge; can be short or long; used on women's and children's peasant blouses.

petal
Short, one-piece sleeve cut with curved edge to form a flower-petal shape; popular on women's and children's garments.

puff
Short, full sleeve with gathers at armhole and hem edge; frequently hem edge is held by a fitted band; popular on girls' dresses and women's garments.

raglan
Sleeve and shoulder section cut as one piece and attached to garment body with an angular seam; used on men's, women's, and children's apparel.

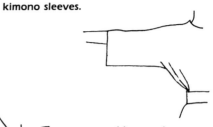
kimono sleeves.

Juliet *or*
Juliette sleeve.

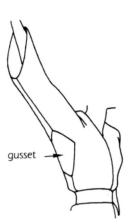
gusset
kimono sleeve with gusset.

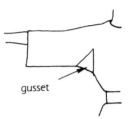
kimono sleeve.

gusset
kimono sleeve with gusset.

lantern sleeve.

melon sleeve.

leg-o'-mutton sleeve.

peasant sleeve.

petal sleeve.

puff sleeve.

raglan sleeve.

roll-up
A straight sleeve that is rolled to the desired length.

set-in
Any shaped sleeve attached to the natural armhole.

shirtwaist
Tailored long sleeve with small gathers or tucks at the wrist, held by a cuff; used on women's, children's, and men's shirts and blouses; frequently sewn with flat-felled seams; also called tailored or shirt sleeve.

tailored
See *shirtwaist*.

trumpet
See *bell*.

sleeve cuffs
A band of fabric used to finish sleeve edge. May be attached to sleeve or be detachable. Types include:

barrel Single band, generally used on shirts, blouses, and dresses.

cavalier Wide, turned-back cuff that is narrow at wrist and flares wide at edge; also called a gauntlet.

French Turned-back cuff held with a cuff link through all four layers of fabric.

sleeve lengths

roll-up sleeve.

set-in sleeve.

shirtwaist sleeve.

barrel cuff.

cavalier cuff.

French cuff.

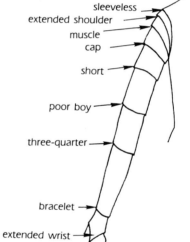

sleeveless
extended shoulder
muscle
cap
short
poor boy
three-quarter
bracelet
extended wrist

sleeve lengths.

balmacaan.

box coat.

car coat.

capes.

chesterfield.

chubby coat.

coachman coat.

cutaway coat.

leggings.

maxi coat.

overcoat
See *topcoat.*

pea
See *pea* jacket, under *Jacket, Section 2.*

polo
Classic straight-line coat with or without buttons and sash; can be single or double breasted; usually made of camel, vicuna, or camel-colored wool fabric. Worn by men, women, and children.

poncho
Rectangular, square, circular, or other geometrically shaped fabric with a slit cut for the head; sometimes has front opening; fabric used can be a blanket type, knitted, or crocheted. Worn by men, women, and children.

princess
Fitted coat cut in long panels from neckline to hemline with no seam at waistline; hemline flares; usually single breasted; popular in the 1950s for women and girls.

reefer
See *pea* jacket, under *Jacket, Section 2.*

slicker
Classic box-style coat made of brightly colored waterproof vinyl; frequently has metal clips as fasteners; worn by men, women, and children.

stadium *or* **suburban**
See *car.*

stole
A rectangle of fabric or fur that wraps around the body without sleeves; sometimes has slits for the arms. Commonly worn by women.

sweater
See *sweater, Section 2.*

tent
Pyramid-shaped coat worn by women in the 1930s, 1940s, and mid-1960s.

toggle
Car coat with wooden or metal toggles used for closing; sometimes has hood; popular for children, and a sporty classic coat for men and women.

topcoat
Any style coat worn by men over a suit; also called an overcoat.

trench
Classic coat used by men and women for rain protection; usually double breasted; has epaulets, loose shoulder yoke, slotted pockets, and buckled belt.

wrap
Straight body coat with fabric tie and no buttons; popular with women in the 1970s.

polo coat.

poncho.

princess coat.

slicker.

stole.

tent coat.

toggle coat.

trench coat.

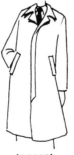

topcoat.

wrap coat.

Coat Fabrics

The fabrics defined in this section are heavyweight, used for coats or jackets.

gabardine
Durable, heavyweight fabric constructed of the twill weave using wool or woollike synthetic fibers. Diagonal ribs can be slight or pronounced depending on the type of yarn used. Much heavier than bottom-weight gabardine.

imitation fur
Made to look like genuine fur by catching synthetic fibers into a knitted background. The fur fibers are usually made of modacrylic fiber, the background of cotton fiber.

melton
Closely woven, heavyweight fabric that has been fulled (a shrinkage process) so it looks like felt.

shearling
Genuine sheared sheepskin or synthetic fibers used to imitate the short, wooly texture. Used in linings of coats or as outside material.

Furs

The pelt of an animal that has been dressed with the hair attached. Furs are used for a variety of apparel and accessories, most frequently for coats and other outerwear.

calf
The pelt of young cattle has flat, short, stiff hair; may be brown in color or black and white, all black, or brown and white. Used for trimmings, accessories, shoes, and vests; moderately durable.

chinchilla
Very delicate, silky haired fur, usually blue-gray with white and darker stripes. Very expensive and very perishable.

fox
Lustrous, long, guard hairs and deep, dense fur fiber. Very popular for stoles, capes, coats, hats, muffs, jackets, and coat collars. Semidurable wearing quality. The four main types of fox include red fox (including black, silver, platinum and cross fox—yellow with black cross marking), white fox, gray fox, and kit fox (small buff-gray).

fur seal
Pelts are sheared to give a soft velvety fur that is usually dyed black or brown. Used for coats, jackets, hats, and muffs. Very durable and very expensive.

lamb
Pelts from lamb have different characteristics. The various types are broadtail (flat fur with moiré design; taken from very young lambs), caracul (lamb with moiré pattern), and Persian lamb (has curly lustrous texture). Persian lamb is pictured. All types of

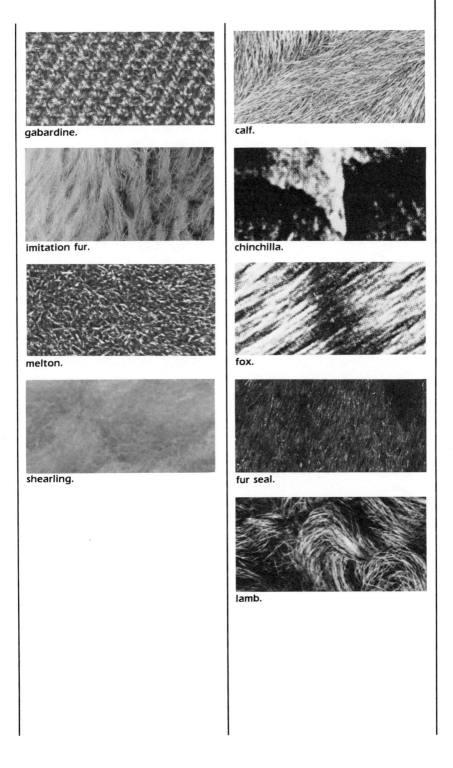

gabardine.

calf.

imitation fur.

chinchilla.

melton.

fox.

shearling.

fur seal.

lamb.

lamb are used for coats and accessories. Very durable or durable depending on the type.

lynx
Dense fur fiber with long, silky, guard hair; ranges in color from creamy white to shadings of pale blue-gray or yellow-brown. Fair durability.

mink
The most frequently worn of all furs because of its excellent durability and wide range of natural or dyed colors. The silky guardhairs and soft fur fiber give it a luxurious hand.

muskrat
Moderate to high durability makes this a popular fur, which can be processed in one of three different ways. Long guard and dense fur fiber are either dyed and striped to look like mink and sable, sheared and dyed to imitate Alaskan seal (this type pic-tured), or left natural and then finished to improve coloring.

rabbit
A very commonly used fur because it is inexpensive and has a soft light texture. May be used in its natural state or dyed and sheared to resemble other furs. Semiperishable.

raccoon
Long or medium length fur that is sometimes sheared for a velvetlike appearance. Brown-gray in color, with light, silvery highlights. Very durable and moderately priced. Full-length coats popular for college students in 1920s and 1930s.

sable
Long, silky guard hairs and soft, dense, fluffy fur fiber; generally used in its natural black-brown color. Looks very similar to mink but is less durable and very expensive.

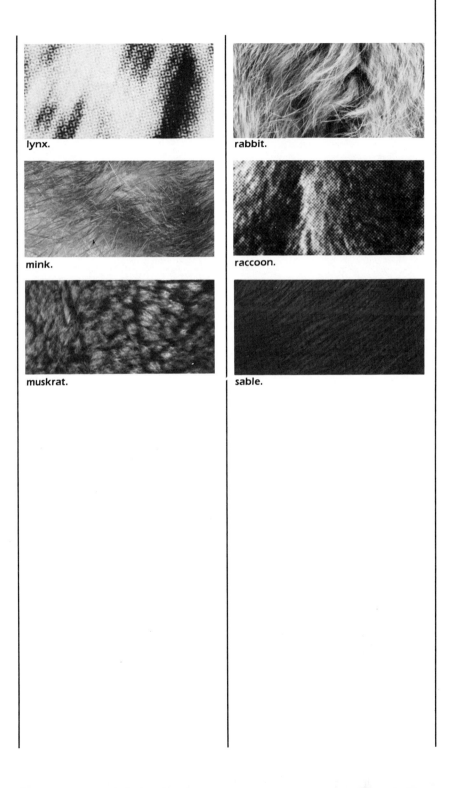

lynx.

rabbit.

mink.

raccoon.

muskrat.

sable.

7
Dresses

Dresses
Dress Fabrics

Dresses

Body coverings generally worn by women and children. A dress consists of a top portion (bodice) and skirt section with or without a definite waistline.

A-line
Outline of dress looks like the letter A, gently flaring at hemline. Introduced by designer Christian Dior in 1955 and very fashionable during 1960s. Also called skimmer and shift.

baby-doll
Fitted bodice and very full skirt made full with many layers of petticoats or hoops. Popularized by American designer Ann Fogarty during the 1950s.

ball gown
An elaborate evening dress of any style.

bib
Popular style for young girls. Has separate "bib" section sewn into the bodice.

bloomer
Frilly bodice and matching short, full, ruffle pants; very popular classic for infants and young girls.

blouson (bloo-*sohn*)
Any style bodice with fullness just below waistline. Popular in the 1920s, 1950s, and late 1970s.

bouffant
See *baby doll*.

bridal
See *wedding*.

caftan
Huge rectangle with openings for arms and neck; adapted from Near Eastern costumes. Fashionable in late 1960s and 1970s. Street-length versions worn as daytime dress, floor length worn for formal or informal at-home wear.

chemise
No-waistline, straight-line dress with gentle flare at hemline. Made fashionable in 1957 by French designer Hubert Givenchy, and revived in the 1980s with pleats the length of dress. Also called a float dress and pencil dress.

christening
Sheer, lightweight long dress worn by infants when they are christened; usually has lace trim. Traditional styles are 6 to 12 inches longer than the baby.

coat dress
Single- or double-breasted front opening similar to a coat; frequently made in heavy fabrics. A classic since 1930; very popular in 1960s, 1970s and 1980s.

cocktail
Any short dress generally worn for late afternoon and evening functions. Popular name in 1950s, 1960s, and 1980s.

cocoon
Big oval shape usually cut on the bias and wraps the body; popular in late 1970s.

drop waist
Elongated bodice with full skirt, frequently dirndl. Fashionable in the 1950s and 1980s.

elasticized waist
Any style dress with a natural elasticized waistline for comfort. Popular in the 1970s and 1980s.

A-line dress.

baby-doll dress.

ball gown.

bib dress.

bloomer.

blouson dress.

caftan.

chemise.

christening dress.

coat dress.

cocktail dress.

cocoon dress.

drop waist dress.

elasticized waist dress.

empire
Dress with waistline under the bust. First introduced by Empress Josephine of France in 1804. Very popular in 1910s and 1960s; a classic style, particularly for formal wear.

fishtail
Very slim dress body with full back, usually ruffled at ends and cut with a slit in front. Fashionable in the late 1940s and the 1970s.

flapper
Named after young women of the 1920s who wore short-skirted dresses with fringes or sequined panels that "flapped" while they danced. Adaptations popular in the 1960s.

float
See *chemise.*

granny
Long dress with full skirt, fitted bodice, high stand-up collar, short or long sleeves; originally made of calico-print fabric. Introduced in California in the 1960s as a beach dress. Popular in the 1970s as a prom dress.

housedress
Popular word used to describe dresses worn while doing houseowwork, especially in the 1950s and early 1960s. Style was usually loose fitting and made of inexpensive woven fabric.

jumper
Sleeveless, collarless, loose-fitting dress generally worn with blouse or sweater underneath.

longuette
Term used in the early 1970s to describe a dress with hemline between knee and floor.

maternity
Dress with fullness in the front; designed for pregnant women.

mushroom
Slim dress with short full overskirt. Popular in the late 1940s and the 1950s.

muumuu (*moo*-moo)
Adapted from the dresses worn on Pacific Islands; flows loosely from front and back yoke; can be ankle or street length; usually made of a colorful Hawaiian print. Popular in the late 1960s and early 1970s.

one-shoulder
Long dress with one bare shoulder; top section is frequently cut on the bias grain of fabric. A classic style, popular in the 1970s and 1980s.

pagoda
Pleated, tiered dress usually made without sleeves and with shoulder straps.

pants dress
Combination bodice with culotte or split skirt bottom. Popular in the 1960s and 1980s. Longer-length version used for evening.

peasant
Bodice with drawstring neck, puff sleeve, lace-up corselet-type vest; skirt is usually gathered into natural waistline with gathered ruffle trim at hem. Derived from European peasant costume. Fashionable in the late 1970s. Called "country look" in the 1980s.

pencil
See *chemise.*

empire dress.

fishtail dress.

flapper dress.

granny gown.

housedress.

jumper.

longuette.

maternity dress.

mushroom gown.

muumuu.

one-shoulder gown.

pagoda dress.

pants dress.

peasant dress.

peplum
Slim silhouette with slightly flared hip-length overskirt. Popular for women in the 1940s and revived in 1970s.

pinafore
Bib-top apron with ruffled shoulder strap and complete full skirt. Worn over a basic dress; frequently made of white-eyelet fabric. Popular for young girls.

prairie
Similar to the peasant costume but less ornate. Fashionable term of the 1980s.

princess
Classic style with seams that extend from shoulder or bustline to hemline without waist seam.

sari *or* saree (*sah*-ree)
Adapted from the Hindu woman's dress. Has ankle-length skirt, short bodice (choli), and transparent rectangle wrapped around the waist with one end thrown over the shoulder. Rectangle frequently trimmed with embroidered gold threads. Traditional dress in India, popular in America in the 1970s.

sarong
Strapless top and wraparound skirt made of coordinating fabric; fabric is often a Polynesian print. First made popular in the 1930s by actress Dorothy Lamour; revived in the 1970s.

sheath
Slim, fitted dress without waistline seam and fitted darts at waist. Fashionable in the 1950s and early 1960s.

shift
See *A-line*.

shirtwaist
Tailored shirt that extends to street-length dress or long evening dress; skirt section may be straight or full. Introduced in the 1930s, very popular in the 1940s, 1950s, and 1970s, and now a classic.

skimmer
See *A-line*.

strapless
Bodice made without shoulders or straps and usually with a wired foundation underneath; mitts frequently worn with formal dress. Fashionable in the 1950s and 1980s.

sundress
Dress with camisole or swimsuit-type top. Introduced in the 1930s; now a classic for summer wear.

sweater dress
Soft knitted dress with or without a waistline seam. A classic style.

tent
Very full, pyramid-shaped dress. Fashionable in the late 1960s.

tiered
Layers of ruffles from bodice to hem. Fashionable in the 1960s and 1980s.

trapeze
Full, unstructured dress with narrow shoulders; hem flares slightly more than A-line. Fashionable in the late 1950s and early 1960s.

T-shirt
Knitted shirt extended to street-length hemline and usually belted. Popular in the 1970s and 1980s.

peplum dress.

pinafore.

prairie dress.

princess dress.

sari *or* saree.

sarong.

sheath dress.

shirtwaist dress.

strapless gown.

sundress.

sweater dress.

tent dress.

tiered gown.

trapeze dress.

T-shirt dress.

tunic
Two-piece dress with elongated top; skirt is usually narrow. Fashionable in the 1960s and 1980s.

wedding
Any style dress worn by the bride for the marriage ceremony. The traditional wedding dress is made of white satin, organza, or similar fabrics and lace with or without a train in back. A veil is generally worn with a headdress.

wrap
Dress fastens by one side crossing over another, and is held with button or tie. Popularized in the 1970s by American designer Diane von Furstenberg.

Dress Fabrics

The fabrics defined in this section are used for dresses as well as other apparel.

batiste
See *Top-weight Fabrics, Section 2.*

butcher linen
Plain-weave, medium-weight fabric with slightly irregular coarse yarns. Made from flax fiber or synthetic fibers made to look like flax.

challis
Supple, lightweight fabric made of plain weave with slightly brushed yarns; usually printed.

crepe
See *Top-weight Fabrics, Section 2.*

dotted swiss
See *Top-weight Fabrics, Section 2.*

eyelet
Lightweight woven fabric with holes punched out and embroidery worked around the hole.

interlock
See *Top-weight Fabrics, Section 2.*

metallic jersey
Single-knit fabric with metallic yarns used in combination with other fiber yarns. Frequently used in evening gowns.

surah
See *Top-weight Fabrics, Section 2.*

sweater knit
Lightweight to medium-weight single-knit fabric usually formed with knit stitches on the face and purl stitches on the back. Some sweater knits have a rib pattern formed by alternating knit and purl stitches on both sides of the fabric.

tunic.

wedding gown.

wrap dress.

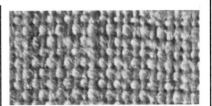

butcher linen.

challis.

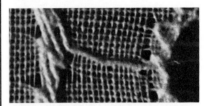

eyelet.

metallic jersey.

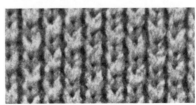

sweater knit.

8

Loungewear and Sleepwear

Nightgowns
Pajamas
Robes
Fabrics

Nightgowns

Loose garment of varying lengths worn for lounging or sleeping by women and children. Styles vary in fabric and details.

granny gown
Long-length gown with high neck, long sleeves, and ruffle-trimmed yoke; usually has ruffle at hem.

nightshirt
Another word for nightgown or gown with shirt styling. Popular styles include T-shirts or man-tailored shirt. Worn by men, women, and children.

shortie
Short nightgown.

Pajamas

Loose-fitting garment worn by men, women, and children for lounging or sleeping. Sometimes called p.j.'s or jammies.

baby doll
Short, full top with short puffy sleeves and short full matching panties. Worn by women and young girls.

blanket sleeper
One or two-piece pajama made of heavy, napped, blanketlike fabric. Generally worn by children.

bunny suit
See *Dr. Denton sleepers.*

Chinese
Two-piece pajama; top is hip length with frog-front closing, mandarin collar, and side slits; pants have straight legs. Frequently made of satin fabric. Worn by women.

cossack
Tunic top with side closing and stand-up collar, worn over straight-leg long pants. Fashionable in the 1930s and late 1960s.

creeper
One-piece, footed pajama with gripper front closings. Usually made of terry cloth or lightweight jersey knit and worn by infants.

Dr. Denton sleepers
One-piece knitted pajama with covered feet, button front, and buttoned drop seat in back. Trade name for this style introduced in 1895 for infants and toddlers; now also made for adults. Also called bunny suits.

nightgown.

granny gown.

nightshirt.

shortie.

baby doll.

blanket sleeper.

Chinese pajama.

cossack pajama.

creeper.

Dr. Denton sleepers.

footed pajama
One- or two-piece pajama with foot covering attached. Foot coverings usually have nonskid vinyl bottoms. Commonly worn in cold weather by children as well as adults.

harem
Very-wide-leg pants gathered at ankles and teamed with a brief top or tunic top. Fashionable for loungewear in the late 1960s.

shortie
Short-length top and short pants of many different styles; worn by men, women, and children.

ski
Two-piece, warm, knit pajama consisting of pullover top and pull-on pants with ribbed knit at neck, wrists, and ankles. Worn by men, women, and children.

tailored
Box-shaped top with man-tailored collar and short or long straight-leg bottoms. A classic style for men, women, and children.

Robes

Loose garment usually worn over sleep or loungewear. May be hip to floor length and have short or long sleeves.

bathrobe
Name given to coverup worn by men and women over lounge and sleep wear. Can be wraparound or front-button style. Length varies from knee to floor length.

beach
See *bathing suit coverup, Active Sportswear, Section 1.*

bed jacket
Short-length jacket usually worn over a nightgown by women while sitting up in bed. Very fashionable in the 1920s and 1930s.

brunch coat
Loose-fitting garment ranging from knee to full length with front closing of buttons, snaps, or zippers. Usually worn by women. Term popular in 1950s. Also called duster or housecoat.

duster
See *brunch coat.*

happi coat
Hip-length jacket with wide kimono sleeve, collarless neckline, and soft self-fabric belt. Usually made of brightly colored satin, frequently bearing a bird, dragon, or medallion embroidered on the back. Used by men and women for at-home wear. Popular in the 1970s.

hostess
Full-length flowing robe worn by women for home entertaining. Usually made of exotic fabric; zips up the front.

footed pajama.

harem pajama.

shortie pajama.

ski pajama.

tailored pajama.

bathrobe.

bed jacket.

brunch coat.

happi coat.

hostess coat.

housecoat
See *brunch coat.*

kabuki
See *happi coat.*

kimono
Patterned after the national dress of the Japanese. Long, loose robe features collarless neckline, wide kimono sleeve, and tie at waist with obi belt. A popular loungewear item in the 1970s.

negligee (*neg*-li-zhay)
Long, flowing, sheer robe usually trimmed with lace, ruffles, or other trim and worn by women over a matching nightgown. Also called a peignoir.

peignoir (pen-*wa*)
See *negligee.*

wrapper
See *bathrobe.*

Fabrics

The fabrics described in this section are used for loungewear, sleepwear and other apparel.

chiffon
See *Top-weight Fabrics, Section 2.*

crepe
See *Top-weight Fabrics, Section 2.*

crepe back satin
Fabric with pebbly surface (face) and shiny smooth back. Usually made of filament yarns of silk or synthetic fibers.

flannelette
Light- to medium-weight soft fabric with brushed surface. Usually made of plain weave from cotton or cotton-blend fibers.

fleece
Woven or knitted fabric with soft napped surface. Usually made of cotton or synthetics such as modacrylic, acrylics, or polyester.

lace
See *Undergarment fabrics, Section 9.*

organdy
See *Top-weight Fabrics, Section 2.*

satin
See *Bottom-weight Fabrics, Section 3.*

tricot
See *Undergarment Fabrics, Section 9.*

kimono.

negligee.

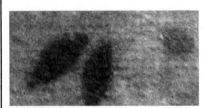

crepe back satin.

flannelette.

fleece.

9

Under-
garments

Bras
Foundations
Girdles
Slips and Petticoats
Underpants
Undergarment Fabrics

Bras

An undergarment used to mold and support women's breasts. Some are very rigid, shaped with bones, wires, and padding; others are soft and flexible. Bras were first introduced in the 1920s. Other names include brassiere and bandeau.

contour
Bra padded with foam or fiberfill.

decolleté (day-kol-eh-*tay*)
Low-cut bra that is usually wired at bottom for support. Worn under low-cut dresses.

demi
Bottom half opaque and wired for support; top half sheer and low cut. Worn with low-cut necklines.

leisure
Unstructured bra of lightweight lacy fabric. Designed for at-home wear or for sleeping.

long-line
Bra extends to waistline. Designed to hold in rib cage and support breasts.

pasties
Decorative cups or coverings over the nipple and or breast area; usually glued on. Worn by exotic dancers.

plunge
Low-cut bra with V-shaped front section. Worn under low-cut necklines.

strapless
Bra made without straps. One style is very stiff and has wires under cups; fashionable in the 1940s and 1950s. The 1970s popular style has soft tricot fabric elasticized at top and bottom, and no wires are used.

stretch
See *leisure*.

wired
Any style bra with wires under cups for support.

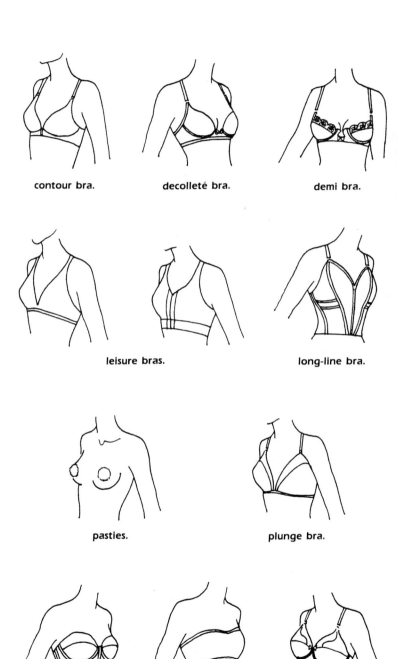

contour bra.

decolleté bra.

demi bra.

leisure bras.

long-line bra.

pasties.

plunge bra.

strapless bras.

wired bra.

Foundations

One-piece bra and girdle or panty combination. Originally a part of woman's dress but now usually a separate undergarment.

boned
Foundation with metal strips (called bones) encased in cotton tape and secured under bust and in various vertical positions from top of bra to hem. Foundation is usually made of woven nonstretch cotton fabric.

lace
Foundation with lace-up closure. Used today for support foundations and decorative ones.

panty
Bra-and-panty combination with a crotch; usually made of knitted two-way stretch fabric.

stretch
See *panty*.

torsolette
Form-fitting hip-length foundation; usually strapless and frequently with garters attached.

zippered
Foundation with zipper closure. Zipper can be located at center front or at sides.

Girdles

Form-fitting garment usually worn by women to mold lower portion of the body. Most are made today of two-way stretch elastic.

boned
Girdle with metal strips encased in cotton tape; usually made of firm-woven fabric. Used by men and women who need firm support.

Capri
Stretch-type panty girdle with legs extending below the knee. Usually worn by women under tight-fitting pants.

Crisscross
One side laps over the other to permit easy walking and sitting. Trademark name of Playtex Corporation.

garter belt
Wide band, approximately 4 to 8 inches, made of woven or lacy fabric; worn by women to hold up stockings.

laced
Firm support girdle with lace enclosure at sides, back, or front. Usually made of firm woven fabric and used by men and women for corrective support.

panty
Stretch girdle with crotch. Length varies from hip joint to ankle.

pull-on
Stretch girdle that is pulled on. No zippers or lacings. The most popular type of girdle used today.

zippered
Girdle with zipper closing to aid putting it on.

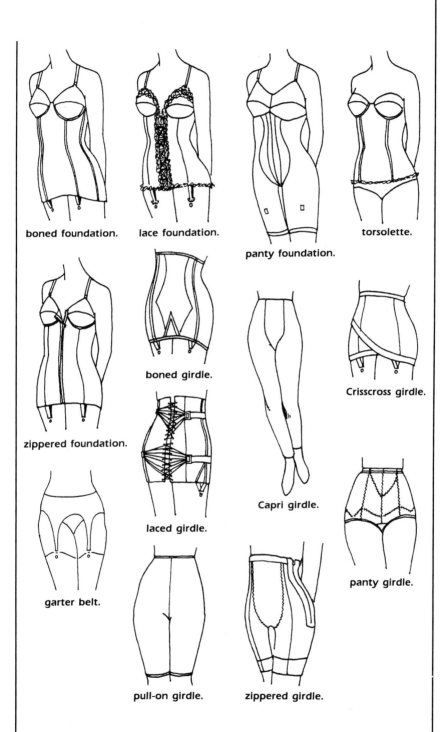

boned foundation.

lace foundation.

panty foundation.

torsolette.

zippered foundation.

boned girdle.

Capri girdle.

Crisscross girdle.

garter belt.

laced girdle.

panty girdle.

pull-on girdle.

zippered girdle.

Slips and Petticoats

Undergarment that acts as a lining. Worn under dresses by women and children. Usually made of lightweight fabric.

bra slip
One-piece bra-and-slip combination. Top section is fitted and frequently strapless. Popular in the 1960s, 1970s, and 1980s.

camisole
Square-neck top slip worn under sheer blouses. Frequently trimmed with lace. Also called a chemise. Popular in the 1950s and 1980s.

chemise
See *camisole.*

crinoline
Very full half slip that has been stiffened. Frequently made of horsehair and sometimes wired with hoops. Fashionable in the 1950s. Used today with square-dance and bridal attire.

full
One-piece bra-and-petticoat combination. Hem length can vary from above the knee to the floor.

half
Slip covers body from waist to hemline.

skivvy
See *undershirt.*

teddy
One-piece camisole-and-panty combination. Frequently made of very sheer fabric and trimmed with lace. Popular in the late 1970s and 1980s.

undershirt
Knitted undergarment worn by men and young children. Styles vary in neckline and sleeve treatment. Also called skivvy or skivvies.

bra slip.

camisole.

crinoline.

full slip.

half slip.

teddy.

undershirts.

Underpants

Undergarments that cover the torso below the waist. Usually called panties when worn by women and girls. Men's underpants are called B.V.D.'s, underwear, drawers, or by their style or brand name.

band leg
Edge of leg is trimmed with a rib-knit band. Used on men's, children's, and women's underpants.

bikini
Edge line begins below the navel. Used by women, young girls, and slim-figured men. Very popular in the 1970s and 1980s.

bloomers
Very full underpants worn by women and girls. Named for Amelia Jenkins Bloomer, nineteenth-century American feminist who wore long, full pants under a short skirt. Popular since 1920s for young girls and fashionable in the 1930s for women. The term is used today as another word for womens' and girls' underpants.

boxer shorts
Square-legged underpants usually made of woven fabric. Men's version has fly front.

brief
Short, body-hugging underpants worn by men, women, and children.

drawers
Ankle- or knee-length fitted underpants worn by men and women, particularly during cold weather and under ski garments. Also called long-johns. Term also used to describe all types of underpants.

flared-leg
Wide leg pants worn by women. Popular in the 1930s and 1940s.

long-johns
See *drawers*.

pettipants
Wide-leg underpants of knee or below length. Frequently worn by women under culotte skirts.

thermal
Styled like drawers and made of fleece-backed knit. Popular for men, women, and children during cold weather.

band leg underpant.

bikini pant.

bloomers.

boxer shorts.

briefs (men's and women's).

drawers.

flared-leg underpant.

pettipants.

Undergarment Fabrics

The fabrics described in this section are used for undergarments.

lace
A category of open-work fabrics produced by weaving, knitting, looping, or interlacing yarns. Made of cotton, nylon, or silk fibers.

power net
Knit fabric produced on a raschel warp knit machine with elasticized yarns. Used for girdles and parts of bras.

satin
See *Bottom-weight Fabrics, Section 4.*

tricot
Stable knit fabric made on a tricot warp knit machine from filament yarns. Fibers include nylon, polyester, or acetate.

lace.

power net.

tricot.

10

Historic
Silhouettes

Antiquity
through
1980s

Historic Silhouettes

Styles are repeated throughout history. A brief glimpse of the history of fashion shows how the individual categories were put together to create a total "fashion look" for a particular period in history.

woman of ancient Crete
Cretan civilization reached its peak from 2800 to 1200 B.C. Skirt was made of tiers of leather. Breasts were bare and supported by a wide belt called a *girdle*. Sometimes the Cretan women covered their heads with small turbans. Cretan women loved jewels and ornaments and used them lavishly.

man of ancient Crete
A very slim waist was typical of the Cretan man, who dressed quite simply. A leather apron was worn over a loincloth. Sandals were worn if he did not go barefoot.

woman of ancient Egypt
Tight-fitting dress of various styles was called a *kalasiris* and usually made of linen fabric. The dress was accessorized with a wig, heavy makeup, and rich jewelry. Jewelry included large bib necklaces and arm and ankle bracelets.

man of ancient Egypt
Men were usually more elaborately dressed than women. A popular attire for noblemen was a pleated kilt and draped headdress called a *klaft.*

woman of ancient Greece
Men's and women's costumes were very similar and often shared to economize. Two rectangles form the basis of each dress, which was belted and draped to give many variations. Sandals were worn on the feet. Greek women loved jewelry and would adorn themselves with bracelets, necklaces, earrings, and rings on fingers and toes.

man of ancient Greece
The Greek warrior wore a kilt made of leather and a metal chest plate. He armed himself with shield and sword.

woman of ancient Rome
Costume very similar to Greek woman. Used draped dress of various shapes. Braids and veil headdress very popular for the hair.

man of ancient Rome
Long or short dress worn under a rectangular stole called a *toga.* A stripe of various colors was used at edge of toga to indicate the wearer's status.

medieval woman
Costume worn from 476 to 1500 A.D. Styled very simply, it concealed most of the body. Overdress, called a *surcoat,* was originally worn by knights and adapted for women.

medieval man
Masculine attire featured a short tunic, usually belted, long breeches, hose or tights, and leather sandals. A long cloak was added for protection in bad weather.

Gothic woman
Costume of the late medieval period was designed to emphasize the human figure. Fur frequently trimmed court costumes worn by aristocratic women. The headdress was called a *hennin.* A woman's social status was revealed by the height of her hennin; some were thirty-six inches high.

Gothic man
Male costume of this period usually consisted of a short tunic worn over

woman of ancient Crete.

man of ancient Crete.

woman of ancient Egypt.

man of ancient Egypt.

woman of ancient Greece.

man of ancient Greece.

woman of ancient Rome.

man of ancient Rome.

medieval woman.

medieval man.

Gothic woman.

Gothic man.

a tight-fitting body suit. The shoe, called *poulaine,* had a long, pointed toe. A man indicated his social status by the length of the point; the longer the point, the higher the status.

Renaissance woman

The Renaissance, which stretched through the fifteenth and sixteenth centuries, was a time of revival in the fine arts. The ideals of the Renaissance were carried over to clothing. Women's costumes broadened from the Gothic period. Rich heavy fabrics were used to create the silhouette. Dresses were cut to emphasize the bosom.

Renaissance man

Knee-length tunic, called a *doublet,* was main garment worn by men. Doublet had wide opening at armhole through which a wide puff sleeve passed.

Elizabethan woman

This very ornate costume featured a small fitted waist, a wide skirt created with a *farthingale* slip (wire-hoop slip) and a high, wired collar often decorated with jewels.

Elizabethan man

The doublet was form fitting and worn over tights or short puff-leg pants. Large brim hat and cape were used to accessorize the costume.

seventeenth-century woman

The farthingale was abandoned, and a split overskirt became fashionable. Large lace collar trimmed the dress. Curly hair wigs were worn by men and women.

seventeenth-century man

Male dress was very effeminate, with touches of lace and ruffles. The male that dressed with breeches tucked into low-heel shoes and a wide-brimmed, plumed hat was known as a *cavalier.*

Puritan woman

The costume worn by early settlers in America was quite simple and very functional. Wide white collars and cuffs trimmed the austere dress.

Puritan man

The male costume usually included a long, doublet top trimmed with white collar and cuffs. Stockings were tucked under knee-length breeches. Wide-brim hat similar to women's hat was also worn.

eighteenth-century woman

The wide hoop skirt returned during this century, but it differed from the farthingale hoop. A *pannier (pan* yay) hoop, which contained wires at sides and flat fabric strips in front, was worn under the wide skirt. Some skirts were three to four feet wide. The pannier made it possible for women to go through doorways sideways and to sit down. Ruffles, laces, and bows were used lavishly to decorate court costumes. Decolleté necklines, powdered wigs, and fans were fashionable.

eighteenth-century man

Fashion historians often describe the male dress of this period as the most effeminate in history. Ruffles, lace, and rich embroidery were used to decorate the costume. A lace ruffle, called a *jabot,* was frequently worn at the neck. The tri-corn hat was also fashionable.

Renaissance woman.

Renaissance man.

Elizabethan woman.

Elizabethan man.

seventeenth-century woman.

seventeenth-century man.

Puritan woman.

Puritan man.

eighteenth-century woman.

eighteenth-century man.

nineteenth-century empire woman (1804–1815)

The rigid ornate dress of the eighteenth century was abandoned for a freer, more natural style. Empress Josephine of France introduced a loose, flowing dress belted under the bustline that became known as the empire (um *peer*) style. The dress was usually worn with a very large stole.

nineteenth-century empire man (1804–1815)

Beau Brummel was the fashion leader who introduced more masculine dress to this era. The attire was characterized by an overly long waistcoat, long-leg trousers, and top hat.

nineteenth-century Romantic woman (1820–1840)

Frills, laces, and bows returned to decorate the wider skirt silhouette made full with layers of petticoats. Corsets were fashionable. The popular sleeve was a leg-o'-mutton for daywear and puff for formal wear.

nineteenth-century Romantic man (1820–1840)

The waistcoat or cutaway coat was introduced during this period. The coat featured a waist-length front and tails in back. Black was a fashionable color for formal wear.

Victorian woman (1840–1870)

Hoops and crinoline petticoats shaped the very full skirt. An extremely tiny waist was fashioned with a torso-length corset. It was fashionable to faint from wearing a very tight corset; some women actually died from wearing a corset that was too tight. Low-cut bodices were in vogue for formal wear.

Victorian man (1840–1870)

Male costume lacked the fussy detail prevalent in women's attire. A plain and practical jacket was fashionable and has remained a basic wardrobe staple for men ever since. The cravat, top hat, and walking stick were stylish accessories.

late-nineteenth-century woman (1870–1890)

Layers of fabric, hoops, and padding were used to create the fullness at back hip area known as the *bustle*. In the 1870s the skirt and bustle were very wide, but by 1890 the silhouette was narrow. Tiny waists and corsets remained fashionable. Fans and parasols were popular accessories. Art nouveau art influenced the wide choice of colors in women's clothes. Color counselors gave women advice on what colors worked best to complement their hair and skin coloring.

late-nineteenth-century man (1870–1890)

Menswear continued to be simple and practical in design. Double-breasted long jackets and topcoats were important basic wardrobe items.

Gay '90s woman

Many styles prevailed in fashion, but one of the most popular was the Gibson girl. Painter Charles Dana Gibson inspired the look, created with high-neck bodice, leg-o'-mutton sleeve, belted waist, and straw sailor hat.

Gay '90s man

The cutaway jacket was the most popular style. It was generally worn over a double-breasted vest with stiff, high-collar shirt, bow tie, and top hat.

turn-of-the-century woman

A silhouette known as the *pouch bosom* was one of the most popular. The silhouette was created by wearing attire with gathers and pleats over the bustline and a fitted waistline. Large wide-brim hats were fashionable.

nineteenth-century
empire woman.

nineteenth-century
empire man.

nineteenth-century
Romantic woman.

nineteenth-century
Romantic man.

Victorian woman.

Victorian man.

late-nineteenth-century woman.

Gay '90s man.

Gay '90s woman.

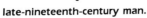

late-nineteenth-century man.

turn-of-the-century woman.

turn-of-the-century man
Many jacket lengths were worn. The jacket lapel was small and buttoned high on chest. High starched collars helped the man hold his head and neck straight. Pants were wide at waist and hips and narrow at the ankles. The derby and fedora were popular accessories.

1920s woman
During the 1920s many radical changes took place in women's clothes. The hemline rose to at or just below the knee. The corset was replaced by the bra. Very fashionable women of this period were known as "flapper girls." Characteristics of the flapper dress include a straight, boyish, almost shapeless silhouette, short skirts, evening dresses with fringes that "flapped," the bob hairstyle, a cloche hat, and a long cigarette holder.

1920s man
Young men had much influence on men's fashion of the 1920s. Daytime apparel had many sporty influences. Popular items included knickers, argyle socks, and saddle oxfords or fringe loafers.

1930s woman
The silhouette of the 1930s was soft and shapely. Many of the styles were created by bias cuts (fabric cut on diagonal grain) introduced by French designer Madeleine Vionnet. Small hats and pumps with platform soles were popular accessories.

1930s man
Menswear featured broad shoulders, double-breasted jackets with wide, low lapels, full-cut pants pleated at the waist, and a trench coat. The fabrics were coarsely textured and very colorful.

1940s woman
Masculine designs influenced women's styles until 1947. The designs included broad, padded shoulders, fitted waist, and slim skirt. Skirt lengths remained short because of fabric shortages during World War II. Small hats worn at the front of the head were popular.

1940s man
British designers influenced much of the fashionable apparel for men. The draped suit that was introduced in the late 1930s continued to be popular. Colors were subdued, with black and navy most frequently used. The double-breasted topcoat was also a fashion favorite. Fabric shortages during World War II created a more slender silhouette.

1950s woman
The baby doll silhouette was most typical of the early 1950s. The silhouette featured natural shoulders, puff or three-quarter straight sleeves, fitted waist, very full skirt made full with layers of petticoats, and midcalf hemline.

1950s man
The single-breasted, natural-shoulder suit with straight, slim lines, known as the "Ivy League look," was the most popular of the decade. The button-down shirt was frequently worn with the Ivy League suit, as were narrow knitted ties.

1960s woman
Radical changes in fashion took place during this decade. A tubular silhouette was the most dominant. Skirt lengths were the shortest in history. Emphasis was on the leg, and textured panty hose were often worn with mini skirts.

turn-of-the-century man.

1920s woman.

1920s man.

1930s man.

1930s woman.

1940s woman.

1940s man.

1950s woman.

1950s man.

1960s woman.

1960s man

The male of the 1960s looked fitter, younger, and more colorful than any other time during the twentieth century. Emphasis was placed at the waistline. A natural shoulder in suit jackets contributed to the long, lean look. The 1960s are often described as the time of the Peacock Revolution because of the extensive use of color.

1970s woman

The radical changes of the 1960s had a profound effect on apparel used by both men and women of the 1970s. Pants were worn by women everywhere: office, church, and social occasions. Many styles were unisex in design, worn by both men and women.

1970s man

Menswear took on a casual look. The leisure suit was popular in the early 1970s. The wash-'n'-wear concept of clothing care, precipitated by technological advances in synthetic fabric design, gained popularity.

1980s woman

A wide range of styles designed to suit the individual dominates the 1980s. Dresses and skirts returned, with a variety of hemlines. Comfort became a characteristic desired by most women, and sportswear became fashionable for both casual and dress wear. Many styles were variations of those popular in the 1940s, 1950s, and 1960s.

1980s man

Comfort and the ensuing widespread adoption of sportswear also had an important influence on male fashion in the 1980s. Business and evening wear became more traditional and conservative in styling than during the 1970s. A slender, natural silhouette dominated.

1960s man.

1970s woman.

1970s man.

1980s woman.

1980s man.

Bibliography

Beaver, Judie. *Fashion Fundamentals*. Austin, Texas: University of Texas, Instructional Materials Services, 1974.

Calasibetta, Charlotte. *Fairchild's Dictionary of Fashion*. New York: Fairchild Books, Inc., 1975.

Crawford, M. D. C. *One World of Fashion*. New York: Fairchild Books, 1967.

Davis, Marian. *Visual Design in Dress*. Englewood Cliffs, New Jersey: Prentice-Hall, Inc., 1980.

Giollo, Debbie Ann. *Fairchild's Designer's Stylist Handbook*. New York: Fairchild Books, Inc., 1980.

————. *Profiling Fabrics—Properties, Performance and Construction Techniques*. New York: Fairchild Books, Inc., 1981.

Kybalova, Ludmila; Herbenova, Olga; and Lamarova, Milena. *The Pictorial Encyclopedia of Fashion*. London: Hamlyn, 1968.

Lessing, Alice; Bower, Rhea; and Stimson, Ermina. *Sixty Years of Fashion*. New York: Fairchild Books, Inc., 1963.

Lynam, Ruth, editor. *Couture*. New York: Doubleday, 1972.

Mathisen, Marilyn Purol. *Apparel and Accessories*. McGraw Hill Book Company, 1979.

Nyberg, Tobi, editor. *The Changing American Woman—WWD—200 Years of American Fashion*. New York: Fairchild Books, 1976.

Peltz, Leslie Ruth. *Fashion: Color, Line and Design*. Indianapolis: Bobbs-Merrill, 1980.

Picken, Mary Brooks. *The Fashion Dictionary*. New York: Funk and Wagnalls, 1973.

Schaeffler, O. E., and Gale, William. *Esquire's Encyclopedia of 20th Century Men's Fashions*. New York: McGraw Hill Book Company, 1973.

Tate, Sharon Lee. *Inside Fashion Design*. San Francisco: Canfield Press, 1977.

Tolman, Ruth. *Guide to Fashion Merchandise Knowledge*. New York: Milady, 1973.

Wingate, Isabel B.; Gillespie, Karen R.; and Milgrom, Betty G. *Know Your Merchandise for Retailers and Consumers*. New York: McGraw Hill Book Company, 1975.

Index

Italics indicate pages with illustrations.

182 | Index